D1050683

THE BEGINNER'S GUIDE TO
WRITING
A NOVEL

If you want to know how . . .

Awaken the Writer Within
Release your creativity and find your true writer's voice

Writing a Children's Book
How to write for children and get published

Creative Writing
Use your imagination, develop your writing skills and get published

The Writer's Guide to Getting Published

howtobooks

Please send for a free copy of the latest catalogue:

How To Books
Spring Hill House, Spring Hill Road,
Begbroke, Oxford OX5 1RX, United Kingdom
info@howtobooks.co.uk
www.howtobooks.co.uk

NEW REVISED AND UPDATED FOURTH EDITION

THE BEGINNER'S GUIDE TO
WRITING
A NOVEL

How to prepare your first book for publication

MARINA OLIVER

howtobooks

Published by How To Books Ltd
Spring Hill House, Spring Hill Road,
Begbroke, Oxford OX5 1RX, United Kingdom.
Tel: (01865) 375794. Fax: (01865) 379162.
info@howtobooks.co.uk
www.howtobooks.co.uk

All rights reserved. No part of this work may be reproduced or stored
in an information retrieval system (other than for purposes of review)
without the express permission of the publisher in writing.

The right of Marina Oliver to be identified as author of this work has
been asserted by her in accordance with the Copyright, Designs and
Patents Act 1988.

© Copyright 2006 Marina Oliver

First published 1996
Second edition 2000
Reprinted 2001
Third edition 2003
Reprinted 2004
Fourth edition 2006
Reprinted 2007

British Library Cataloguing in Publication Data
A catalogue record for this book is available from the British Library

ISBN 978 1 84528 091 8

Cover design by Baseline Arts Ltd, Oxford
Produced for How To Books by Deer Park Productions, Tavistock
Typeset by PDQ Typesetting, Newcastle-under-Lyme, Staffs.
Printed and bound by Cromwell Press, Trowbridge, Wilts.

NOTE: The material contained in this book is set out in good faith for
general guidance and no liability can be accepted
for loss or expense incurred as a result of relying in particular
circumstances on statements made in the book. The laws and
regulations are complex and liable to change, and readers should check
the current position with the relevant authorities before making
personal arrangements.

Contents

List of Illustrations

Preface

to the Fourth Edition

The response to the earlier editions of this book, by both published and unpublished novelists, has been encouraging and enthusiastic. I'm delighted when writers say they find it useful and easy to use.

Since I wrote this book ten years ago the publishing world has changed in several ways, but more importantly, the remarkably rapid spread of access to the Internet has transformed the possibilities for authors – for research, contact with other writers, publishing, sales and self-promotion. Writers who are not online are seriously disadvantaged in many ways. Many agents and editors, for instance, now use email, and expect their authors to do so. There is a wealth of research material available at the click or two of a mouse. Many publishers now demand copies of accepted typescripts on computer disks.

I do not give information on how to be connected, to navigate or use the Net, or general information on what can be found there, as there are plenty of books dedicated to these topics. I have listed a few of the sites I have found useful, in a new Appendix 3, but there are millions of sites already and thousands being added (and deleted) every week. Also names can be sold and one sometimes finds quite different sites to the one expected. Most of the ones I give have useful links elsewhere – they might be called umbrella, or library sites.

All the time the world of publishing, book production and bookselling sees yet more changes, not all of them beneficial to the novelist. More novels are being published each year. New publishers have come (and gone). Digital printing has replaced the older typesetting methods. Supermarkets are selling more books, but of a limited range of titles. Internet bookstores have increased their market share. Electronic publication and print on demand have become more common. Self-publishing is easier and bookstores are more willing to stock these books. Authors have to do more self-promotion.

No doubt there will be more changes in the future, which authors need to be aware of.

Marina Oliver

Acknowledgements

I would like to give heartfelt thanks to the writers and readers – the two ends of the writing business – and the essential intermediaries – the agents, editors, reviewers, librarians, and booksellers – all very busy people, who so generously and frankly answered my questions and gave freely of their knowledge and expertise.

There was a remarkable unanimity of views on many fundamental questions, whether from writers, agents, editors or readers. It will pay intending novelists to heed them. The authority of these people's varied experiences was invaluable, and their ways of expressing ideas much better than mine. I owe them much.

Where I have quoted directly it is because people have agreed that their comments can be attributed, and I have indicated names in brackets after the quotation. A list of names and positions is given in Appendix 1 at the end of the book. I am particularly grateful to Frances Hawkins and the members of the Ruislip Literary Society, and Jill Rundle and the Louth Writers' Circle who answered my questionnaire as groups, thereby increasing the range of answers.

A few people preferred anonymity, so I cannot extend public thanks to them, but they know how grateful I am for their answers.

Many people have recommended Internet sites to me, but I am in particular grateful to Anne Weale, who writes *The Bookseller* column A Bookworm on the Internet for suggesting *The Internet for Writers*, by Nick Daws and for sharing with me many other Internet sites she has discovered. Anna Jacobs, Louise Marley, Indira Hann, Pamela Cleaver, Elizabeth Hadwick, Joan Hessayon, Lindsey Townsend, Carol Wood, Loren Teague, and Benita Brown offered other suggestions and shared their knowledge with me, and if I have missed out anyone, my apologies.

Marina Oliver

Marina is a practising author as well as an editor. She does reports on typescripts for publishers, the Romantic Novelists' Association New Writers' Scheme, as well as her own appraisals agency Storytracks. She has lectured at many writers' courses and conferences.

Foreword

The old adage about writing being ninety-nine per cent perspiration and one per cent inspiration is certainly true. Many a talented writer has failed to achieve full potential because of a lack of perspiration. But having said that one also has to point out that the one per cent inspiration is essential. Without it you cannot begin. In over thirty years of editing I've observed that the inspiration is something you're born with – a mixture of observation and imagination and no amount of hard work can create the gift if it isn't there in the first place.

However, it is quite surprising how many people do have the talent to write, but for a wide variety of reasons manage to hide that talent, in some cases so well that it is hidden from even the most perceptive of editors. Sometimes the talent is obscured by sheer bad English – more of them than you would think! I once had a typescript submitted with an accompanying letter which said, 'dear sir I have writ a book'. Funny, yes, but also sad. There may well have been a talent there, but a busy editor doesn't have the time or patience to wade through an ungrammatical, unpunctuated, mis-spelt typescript. Sometimes the writer is choosing the wrong medium for his or her talent – writing historicals when they should be writing thrillers, or fiction when biographies are their natural métier. The opening lines, paragraphs, chapters can be wrong, disguising the fact that halfway through the book *does* becomes exciting, but how many readers will persevere with a dull book in the hope it will improve? Characterisation, or the lack of it, is a common pitfall. I find I am often telling writers to go away and 'live with their characters' for a time, and then start again. All these things, and many more, can mean that a writer who does have talent, may not make it to the printed page.

Writers *do* need all the help they can get in the way of professional expertise and general advice. Sometimes a friendly editor will spend time on your particular problems, but a good beginning is to read as much as you can about general presentation, plotting, and crafting. The following pages may well pinpoint just what you need to know. Read, adapt, and apply. Then try again. And don't be discouraged. If you have the one percent inspiration, it will eventually win through!

Diane Pearson
Best-selling novelist, editor – Transworld Publisher,
President – The Romantic Novelists' Association

1

Taking Those First Vital Steps

'Some day I think I'll write a novel.' Many people express this wish but do no more. They don't have the burning desire to write which marks really committed writers.

'Everyone has a book in them' is a frequently stated belief. It may be true, but it's the getting it out that matters. This book is designed to help you put your novel on the page in the way that will give you the best chance of selling it. It's not easy, it can be hard work and often disappointing, and luck plays a critical part, but it *is* possible. With persistence, knowledge of your new world, and belief in yourself, you can succeed. The rewards, the delight in achievement, make all the effort worth while.

♦ 'Everyone has a certain amount of talent. Nurture it and keep practising. "Use it or lose it".' (Susan Sallis)

THE REASONS NOVELISTS WRITE
Why do you want to write a novel? Are your reasons the same as those of published novelists?

♦ 'To entertain.' (Ann Hulme, aka Ann Granger)

♦ 'To entertain the reader.' (Andrew Puckett)

♦ 'I want to tell a story, to entertain... like to create a time and place.' (Joan Hessayon)

1

- 'To provide leisure entertainment (and to give myself the pleasure of creation).' (Anne Melville)

- 'To tell a story, and for my own enjoyment, doing something I love.' (Marina Oliver)

- 'To entertain, to excite, to enlighten – but most of all to tell a good story.' (Frederick Nolan)

- 'Apart from the money!! To entertain and amuse, but most of all *to be read.*' (Anita Burgh)

- 'Almost always to tell a story in the way the story itself demands to be told. There are subsidiary aims too, such as: to pay the mortgage, to earn praise.' (Philip Pullman)

- 'To create a world looking from a new angle. A new perspective on the familiar.' (Matthew Kneale)

- 'To offer readers intelligent, and (I hope) entertaining and absorbing escapism from the endless stresses and strains of everyday life. Healthier than tranquilisers!' (Reay Tannahill)

BEING PROFESSIONAL

You want to write a novel, a long work of fiction which entertains, takes readers into an imaginary world. Perhaps you've written one and want to improve it. This book will:

- guide you through the basic techniques
- help you to avoid common pitfalls
- show you how best to present your work.

And 'remember that your first task is to entertain the reader.' (Sarah Molloy)

Behaving like a professional
Many people want to become novelists, but there is a crucial difference between most of them and you. You have made a start, shown a positive interest. You've already made a professional decision by reading this book, so keep on behaving like a professional. Tell yourself every day that you are not a scribbler or dabbler, but a proper writer.

◆ 'Never think of yourself as an amateur – once you put pen to paper you're a writer.' (Anita Burgh)

One definition of professionals is people who are paid for what they do. To get to that position they first have to show certain attitudes, apply standards which distinguish them from the amateur (in the sense of one who does not want to be paid, which does not imply worse in any way).

◆ (I look for) 'evidence that the author has a professional attitude.' (Carole Blake)

Checklist
Professionalism involves:

◆ **Attitudes** – Taking your work seriously.

◆ **Self-discipline** – You don't have a boss to supervise or tell you what to do.

◆ **Determination** – The will to succeed despite setbacks.

- **Time and energy** – You can always find some if you really want to.

- **Commitment** – Putting your writing as a top priority.

Having a professional attitude

As a professional writer you must display the qualities listed above, which are as vital to success as talent. One day, with them, you'll be paid too.

You are going to write a novel. Don't be apologetic or let anyone deter you. Other writers will understand your problems and anxieties so seek them out, talk with them, and most of all learn from them.

Working like a professional

Know what you are doing, creating a product for which there is a market. Authors, **agents** and **editors** create books, and the ultimate demand comes from readers through libraries and bookshops. But in a very real sense agents and editors are intermediary buyers of your product. You are the primary producer, they are the first buyers who process your work into the finished form, so you have to sell to them first. You need to know what they want, as they know what readers want, and be able to supply it on a regular basis. Start off with professional working practices.

- Organise your time and space to obtain the best possible working conditions.

- Budget for expenses as you would for any other business – machinery such as a computer, materials including reference books, paper and postage, running costs such as telephone, subscriptions, training courses and travel.

◆ Be realistic in setting targets and evaluating work. (Tips on how to achieve these aims are given in the book *Starting to Write*, originally published in this series.) The second edition, considerably altered, is available from the author. (See page 176.)

◆ Know your good and bad points, capitalise on the good ones and make allowances for the others while you try to improve them.

◆ Prepare your attack. Don't rush in without doing your research. As with many other tasks, good preparation can save a lot of time later on. Without it your work might need major surgery, or have to be discarded. Or you might not reach the end because you lost your way.

◆ Don't be impatient, and don't give up at the first setback. Professionals persevere.

◆ 'If writing a novel seems like hard work, then you are in the wrong line of business. My first effort was comprehensively rubbished... I immediately sat down and started another.' (Joan Hessayon)

BEING METHODICAL
Targets

Time is valuable, especially when your writing must be fitted in with another job, and this applies to most writers at first. It isn't easy making a living from writing, and it can take several years to build up income. Writers cannot depend on writing income to begin with.

- 'Don't give up the day job until you've really made it.' (Barbara Levy)

If you are a compulsive writer, though, isn't it a wonderful feeling to think your hobby, if approached professionally, could bring in extra income?

How much time?

Don't think there isn't enough time after you've been to the office, or looked after children all day, or have lots of other interests. There is *always* time for writing, if that is your priority and if you give up other things.

To the question 'How much time per week did you spend writing before you were published?' I had the following replies, which show that dedication pays.

- 'a few hours' (Sara Banerji)
- 'eight to ten hours' (Anne Melville)
- 'two, three, four hours per evening five days a week.' (Frederick Nolan)
- 'I wrote all day while my children were at infant school and I didn't have a paid job' (Margaret James)
- 'fifteen hours' (Susan Sallis)
- 'five hours a day' (Joan Hessayon)
- 'I tried to spend at least ten hours' (Andrew Puckett)
- 'I just made time' (Anita Burgh)
- 'every spare moment including while vegetables boiled and babies napped. On bus and train journeys, you name it!' (Ann Hulme)

When?

Decide how much time each day or week you can devote to writing, and promise yourself you will spend that time sitting at your desk and doing the job.

Choose the time when you are most energetic. Many writers get up early to work. Most of the published writers said they did creative work in the mornings.

♦ 'Write every day.' (Philip Pullman)

This is the ideal, but if you genuinely can't, don't despair. Set weekly targets, so that you can catch up if some days you cannot write because of other claims. Longer stretches may suit you better than many brief ones.

♦ 'I work when I can, like to spend several hours at a time on writing a couple of days a week rather than an hour or two daily' (Margaret James).

♦ Keep a diary of your progress.

Thinking time

You need time for thinking too, for planning ahead or taking stock of what you've already done. You can plan the next chapter, work out the plot, get to know your characters. It's as important as getting the words onto paper. It's possible to do at all sorts of odd moments.

Your workplace

When and where you write will depend on circumstances. Try to be regular, to have your own desk always ready for use.

Word processed scripts are essential

When you send your novel to a publisher a word processed script looks more professional. You could manage with a fairly cheap computer, but it's worth the small amount extra to buy one which will give you access to the Internet. Buy the best printer you can afford.

Virtually all professional writers now use word processors, though many begin with pen or pencil for their first draft. But beware. Sarah Broadhurst previews and reviews for *The Bookseller,* amongst other papers and magazines. She must hold the record for seeing the largest selection of new books, dealing with about 1,200 a year and says, 'I believe the word processor has seriously damaged the novel. Authors no longer have to type and retype, which is when a lot of dross was cut out, now it's just moved somewhere else and frequently shows.' If you don't use a word processor you will probably need to have your script word-processed professionally, which is expensive.

Organising your notes

Prepare a filing system to keep your notes, ideas and records where you can find them quickly.

Action points: making plans

1. Determine what time of day is best for your physical writing time.

2. Decide how much time you can devote to writing.

3. Calculate how much time during a typical day you could be thinking about writing while doing something else.

4. Devise an efficient working space, and set it up now.

NOVELS ARE EASIER TO PUBLISH THAN SHORT STORIES

Most fiction writers start with short stories because they take less time than novels. Markets for short stories are a few women's magazines, small specialist magazines and competitions. The supply of short stories is huge.

Fewer people attempt to write novels, yet over 10,000 titles (not all new ones) are published each year, by almost a hundred UK publishers or their individual imprints. Always check addresses and contact details, since editors move jobs, and amalgamations and transfers of owner-ship are happening all the time. There is still competition, of course, but the chances of success are better with a greater demand and smaller supply. There is a list of publishers in Appendix 2, but it is not comprehensive. Look for new ones. They will probably be looking for new authors.

THEY'LL TAKE SO MUCH TIME! A FALLACY

A novel could be 90,000 words long, and a typical short story 1,000 to 3,000 words or fewer. It seems a daunting task, but is it really such a big mountain? If you write a thousand words a day, let's say three pages, an hour's work, you can write a first draft of 90,000 words in three months. You will then have to spend time revising and redrafting, but you can write a novel in a year. When I was a full-time lecturer I often wrote 200,000 or more words a year.

Could you write and sell ninety short stories in a year, finding different plots, new characters and settings?

Action point

Keep a diary for a week or a month, and calculate how much you normally write per hour, then how long it will take you to write 100,000 words.

STUDYING THE MARKET

This is more important than many writers appreciate. It is not so that you can copy what is currently fashionable, but to know what is being published and what the trends are.

- ◆ 'Write what you want to write, from the heart, not what you believe to be fashionable. If you do the latter, by the time you've finished and the novel might be published trends will have moved on.' (Jane Morpeth)

- ◆ 'Please read what else is being published and understand what the publishing industry is looking for and why... It seems to me that the most successful authors are those who are exceptionally clued up about what is happening within the publishing industry and gear their work to those demands.' (Luigi Bonomi)

- ◆ (I often reject) 'writers who are completely out of touch with the market place and who don't themselves seem to read.' (Barbara Levy)

The books

There are different sorts of novels, a whole spectrum from light and frothy, pure entertainment, to the literary heavyweights. They vary in length and in their emphasis on different aspects, but it's possible to group most of them into recognisable types, though the distinctions are more blurred than they were.

The **genres** such as crime, romance, horror, science fiction, westerns and fantasy follow certain conventions and appeal to a restricted readership. So do the 'literary' novels, while 'mainstream' have a more popular, general appeal. There is a growing trend towards the novels which are a cross between commercial and literary. You probably read several types yourself, and can say which genre a book resembles. It's likely you will want to write the sort of book you enjoy reading, so at first concentrate your market research on that type of book.

Action point

Make a list of your ten favourite books, say what type they are and why you enjoy reading them. Which sort do you think you could and would like to write?

The publishers

Some publishers produce a wide variety of novels, others specialise. You are wasting time and money if you send the wrong book to the wrong publisher. If one house publishes, say, only one thriller a year, and that is by one of the most popular thriller writers, they are not likely to accept a new writer of thrillers. A publisher who does a dozen a year might, though.

Book clubs

The growth of these clubs and reading groups has stimulated the demand for books, with an emphasis towards the literary.

Checklist

By making notes of:

- the titles of the books you study
- what sort they are
- what length they are
- what the style of writing is
- who publishes them
- which authors write them

you will begin to see some names repeated.

Action points

1. Make a card or computer index of books you read, with notes on the above. A database could help sort out patterns.

2. Visit publishers' websites and read comments from writers and readers.

The bookshops

- '[Authors] 'need to spend a lot of time in bookshops asking booksellers questions.' (Luigi Bonomi)

Action points: using bookshops for research

1. Spend a long time in a large bookshop. Shops stock the latest publications.

2. The few hardback novels will be the best-sellers and won't be much guide to you.

3. Concentrate on the Top 10 or Top 20 lists, and recent publications.

4. Look at paperback special categories such as crime, best-sellers, popular or twentieth century fiction.

5. Read the blurbs to see what the books are about, and what sort of people might be tempted to read them.

6. Make notes on which publishers are most often represented and which authors have several titles displayed.

Internet bookstores

These are likely to have a vastly larger list than even the biggest high street bookshop. Most of the large sites, such as < *amazon.com* > have reviews of books, so you can see what other readers think of them. Some authors write comments, too.

The libraries

Librarians know a great deal about reading tastes, reviews and publishing trends. Many run reading groups. Talk to them.

◆ Readers will try new types of books 'if we encourage them.' (Margaret Garrett)

Action points: using libraries

1. Read all you can of popular authors and the other, similar books their publishers do.

2. Consult specialist lists such as *The Guardian* annual list of the top hundred 'fast-sellers'.

3. Look at publishers' catalogues and websites to see the range of books they publish.

4. Read the weekly magazine *The Bookseller*, available in most libraries, which has comprehensive review columns.

5. If you don't have Internet access at home most libraries now provide this.

6. You might even visit the London Book Fair, held each year in March, where publishers have display stands and you may have a chance to talk with their staff.

STUDYING THE CRAFT
Reading
Writers must read.

◆ 'Read and read and read and read and read. Read analytically, to see how the successful authors do it (and where they fail).' (Michael Legat)

Read novels and see why some are best-sellers. What do they have in common? Why are they popular?

Read books and articles about the craft of writing. Go to talks by writers. There are numerous day, weekend and longer courses for writers. You may wish to join a class or buy a writers' magazine.

The not-yet-published novelists I spoke to, who had all published other things, belong to groups and read books on writing. 'Most have at least one or two useful ideas – also they all encourage a positive idea.' (Zoë March)

Checklist: analysing what you read
Look at how the authors:

◆ use words
◆ use sentences and paragraphs
◆ introduce characters
◆ convey information about characters
◆ tell you what the conflict is, or the mystery

- describe the setting, the time or place, and technical details such as forensic or legal procedures
- include factual details they will have researched
- use dialogue
- use description
- make characters vivid and memorable
- create tension
- use humour
- vary the pace
- make the most of important scenes
- arouse interest at the start
- maintain interest
- resolve conflicts or puzzles
- tie up loose ends
- finish satisfactorily.

Practising writing

Later in the book you will be given tips on how to do these things yourself. Writing is a craft and can be developed. We don't expect a painter to produce a masterpiece without first learning the techniques and trying them out. Look at every piece of writing you do as something you can learn from. If your submissions are rejected, that's hard, but most writers have experienced it. The successful ones are those who have learned from each lack of success (it isn't a failure, it just didn't win the prize) and go on to do better next time.

DISCUSSION POINTS

Some of these questions at the end of each chapter might form the basis of discussions or exercises at writers' group meetings, or you can consider them independently.

1. Novels can make one of the following the most important feature: the world in which the story is set; the problem to be solved; the relationships of the characters; major events of epic proportions. Find examples of each type.

2. Which type of novel do you want to write, and why? Is it for money or fame, because you have a story to tell, because you enjoy writing, or something else?

3. Do a brief summary (one page only) of a book you like, mentioning the aspects you feel are important, such as plot, characters, dialogue, the way it was written and so on. Then compare this with summaries of other novels.

(2)

Finding the Right Story

LOOKING FOR IDEAS EVERYWHERE

Which comes first, **plot** or **characters**? The answer to this often-asked question is either or neither. You need an idea for lift-off, and this can be a plot, a character, a setting, an incident, a theme, a title, a few words.

Where do you get ideas?

◆ 'There are always ideas – it's a question of which one.' (Susan Sallis)

◆ 'I try and think of lots of things – and hang on to the notions that don't seem stupid.' (Matthew Kneale)

◆ 'Anywhere and everywhere. I got a whole detective story from a few words overheard in a bus queue.' (Ann Hulme)

◆ 'I don't know. They come – some good, some not so good. You judge. You discard. You try. You learn.' (Frederick Nolan)

◆ 'A place, a person, a situation, a setting – something out of which other ideas come, and onto which I can graft more ideas.' (Marina Oliver)

◆ 'From living with and observing people.' (Andrew Puckett)

- 'Triggered off by news items or some personal event.' (Sara Banerji)

- 'Three-line paragraphs in newspapers... Anything will do which presents an interesting situation and prompts the question: "How did they get into this mess and how are they going to get out?"' (Anne Melville)

- My editor suggested that I write novels with some connection to gardening, and this has been the most helpful thing anyone said to me... I have plenty of ideas (but) not all the ideas are good ones... I choose a location and the place suggests a time and the time suggests a plot.' (Joan Hessayon)

Using ideas

All writers have too many ideas, the problem is knowing which make viable stories. You only need one to keep on working, it's the *way* you use ideas that's important.

You may have too few ideas because you are not yet used to recognising them for what they are or might be.

- 'I think when you've been writing for some time you recognise as story ideas thoughts which non-writers probably have just as frequently, but don't recognise because they don't use them.' (Philip Pullman)

Checklist

Find ideas through:

- people you know, see or read about
- places you know, go to, or read about

- major events such as war, terrorism, earthquakes
- historical events
- individual triumphs and tragedies
- phrases overheard
- newspapers and magazine reports of odd or new things people do
- diaries
- advertisements
- agony columns
- newspaper and magazine letter columns
- guide books
- myths, legends and fairy stories
- titles, first lines and quotations.

Ideas emerge from the subconscious, based on things we encounter. We then treat them consciously by bombarding them with information, playing with possibilities, planning how to use them and what we need to research about them.

Action point: asking questions

Whenever you see, hear or read something which might be the germ of an idea, ask the following questions relating to it:

1. **Who** (are they, could they be, lives there)?

2. **What** (are they, do they do, is their nature)?

3. **How** (did it happen, did it get there, could it change)?

4. **When** (did it happen, did they meet, did they part)?

5. **Why** (did it happen then, there, and to them)?

6. **Where** (did it happen, and why there, and how)?

7. **What if** (any number of possibilities occur)?

AN EXAMPLE
Imagine a village with several houses around the green.

What are they? Let's suppose a vicarage, a general shop, an antiques shop, a pub, the home of a rich farmer, a weekender's cottage, cottages of farm labourers, a commuter to London, another to a nearby big town.

Who lives in each? There will be families, babies or teenage children, elderly relatives, *au pairs* or nannies, and they will have relatives and other visitors.

What jobs do they do? Not just the householder, but the rest of the family or the lodgers. Do they have hobbies or passionate interests or obsessions?

Given this wide selection of people, what are their backgrounds? Have they lived here long? What liaisons or quarrels might they have, amongst each other or outside?

What event, such as a newcomer arriving, or a proposal to build a new housing estate, or a sudden tragedy, might spark off a whole series of consequences?

If you haven't, by now, gleaned several ideas, go back and ask further questions, or devise different answers.

Keeping track of ideas

- 'Keep your eyes and ears open and *make notes!* You won't remember.' (Ann Hulme)

Write ideas down and file them. You will soon have far more than you will ever use, but just browsing through them can start the creative process off again.

PLOTTING

What is a plot?

You have had an idea, done some research, made lots of notes, and then perhaps you can't see the way forward or impose any sort of order on your creation. Don't worry. This is a normal part of the creative process.

Let it germinate, let the subconscious take over, and the mass of ideas and facts will begin to take on a shape, make patterns, and you have the basics of a plot. The important ideas and facts will float to the surface, begging to be used. Trust your instinct and take these to work on. Your novel will start to become more real, a concrete idea instead of a hazy mass of unconnected snippets.

Ronald A. Tobias has written an excellent book, *Twenty Master Plots*, in which he analyses the different types of plots under headings such as Adventure, Quest, Transformation. This book is illuminating, and will certainly stimulate ideas.

If you are really stuck there are Internet sites which offer help with developing plots.

Theme

Theme is not the same as plot, it's the impulse behind the plot. It's often an abstract notion like jealousy, revenge, or ambition. It can be more concrete, such as a search, a conflict, or coping with change. Usually it can be described in a few words

A story is not necessarily a plot, though we tend to use the words interchangeably. A story can be a series of events, rather like diary entries. A plot is more.

This happened because

A plot is a series of cause and effect events told in a dramatic way. The actions described have consequences. As the author you are in control in that you are deciding what events are important and showing them in a particular way.

Being original

The events you are relating must be strong, realistic and believable, but different and original.

Don't worry if you cannot find a plot which seems original. It's been said there are only so many plots, though the precise number varies. It's the treatment that matters. Plots are like Lego building blocks – the same limited variety of shapes and colours which can be built up into hundreds of different combinations. If you gave ten people the same basic idea, situation and set of characters you would have ten different plots.

Being believable

Even in fantasy you need to make readers suspend disbelief.

◆ 'I do like a book to catch my imagination somehow, with that magical combination of character and narrative that makes me care what happens even while I know it is fiction.' (Mary Brackley)

Readers know it's unreal, but for the time they are reading they want to believe, and it's up to you to convince them by making your characters real, the plots logical, and the resolutions of crises apparently inevitable. Don't make your characters do impossible things, and remember it's lazy plotting and breaks your implied contract with the reader to get out of difficulties with unforeseeable coincidences, or bringing on the *deus ex machina*, the god who arrives to sort out the mess made by mere mortals.

Devising a plot

Set up the initial situation, the relationships, obsessions and the conflicts. Now, and throughout the book, ask 'What happens next?' You could go off in many directions, but aim to have reasonable, believable developments, yet not the boringly obvious. You want to surprise readers while convincing them that your plot is right and inevitable.

Bring in complications, increase the conflict and intensity, prevent your characters from reaching their objectives too easily. Towards the climax develop the main crisis which is then confronted, have the showdown and get it resolved satisfyingly.

When characters determine plot

At this stage you also need characters who will be the

means of acting out the plot. If you have the right people in the right situations they will to some extent determine the plot through the development, or revelation, or interactions of characters. All the time ask 'What if this happens?' and what different characters would do in particular situations.

You can start with some characters and a situation and see where it leads you, since a complicated story will twist and turn in ways which surprise the author too.

♦ 'I don't plot, I just "go with it".' (Anita Burgh)

Starting with the end
You can alternatively start at the end and plan how to get there. Many, though not all, crime novels start with the ending.

Play on the emotions of readers, make them share the emotions of the characters, but remember that emotion without action is not a plot.

The shape of a plot
A plot progresses through a series of peaks and troughs, high and low points, crises and reflection. There will be lots of small crises, building towards the major one.

You are likely to have subplots which need to be woven in, like a plait. They can be brief, soon resolved, or almost as long as the main plot. They can involve the main characters or minor ones, or both. They need developments, crises and resolutions in the same way as the main plot.

Pre-planning

It is advisable for beginners to draw up an outline of what is likely to happen, to save going too far off track. It could cause months of rewriting if you don't decide beforehand whether your plot can work, whether the time-scale fits in, whether you can get your characters in the right places when you need them there.

Decide which are going to be the big scenes, the crises or turning points of the plot, and plan how you will work up to them. Don't have them too close together, intersperse with minor scenes (see Figure 7, page 96).

If you have only a sketchy plan, though, don't worry. Writers differ enormously in how they work, including how much they plan ahead. Many have little or no idea of what will come next. Many say that when they start they know where they are going, but not the route by which they get there. Others write vast outlines.

♦ 'I start with a full synopsis (forty single-spaced pages of it). Ideas seem to flow more freely in a synopsis, when there are no stylistic problems to slow them down. Though I may depart from the framework when I begin writing, having a proper framework means that I never stray too far.' (Reay Tannahill)

Try to express the basic plot in one sentence.

DOING RESEARCH

Why is this necessary?

'Write what you know.' It would be very restricting if we

all wrote only about our personal knowledge and experience. Most of us have limited experience, but we have imagination. Without this we would have no science fiction, fantasy, historicals, and very few crime books. 'Write what you already know about or can research' is better advice.

Some research is necessary for most novels. You won't know all the details you need, and if you don't know them you won't convince the reader. Many best-sellers are based on vast amounts of research and insider information which the novelist gleans and then portrays dramatically. But beware of dragging in facts which are not relevant to the story and don't carry it forward in some way.

The ideal is to incorporate the details as and when they are relevant, give colour or deeper understanding to the plot or of the characters, but without it being obvious to the reader. The reader should never feel that a fact has been included just because the writer knows it, or finds it interesting.

Readers said that they particularly enjoyed novels which:

- ◆ 'have an element of surprise' (Yvonne Morley)

- ◆ 'have information about the running of a business and work' (Valerie Bennett)

- ◆ 'believe in the story' (Rosemary Guiver)

- ◆ 'are set in a different part of the country/world/age' (Nancy Brazier)

- 'language that is fluent and well expressed' (Anne Donnelly).

Checklist: what you already know
- What jobs have you done?
- What hobbies and interests do you have?
- What countries have you been to?
- Which parts of the UK do you know best?

Where to do it
You don't often need to consult primary sources such as documents and letters in dusty archives, since these have usually been written about by scholars trained to read Latin or archaic handwriting. Read their articles or books.

It does help, though, to see places for yourself, or visit museums and history theme parks, or read contemporary newspaper accounts. You can explore specialist libraries, look at detailed maps, talk to experts, ask public and private organisations for information.

Now the Internet provides endless opportunities for research. Many universities, libraries and museums have their own sites. You can look at maps and documents, pictures, timetables, telephone directories. Perhaps most valuable of all, many sites provide links to or guides of other sources you may never have found or had access to previously. Be wary, though. Anyone can put anything online. Double and triple check, and go to the most authoritative sources.

CDs, DVDs and videos are available too, which give a good idea of how places look, even if they cannot convey the same complete feel of a house or town that an actual visit can.

When to do it

Preliminary research will be needed to help organise your plot and check that it is feasible. It will often provide ideas for characters or incidents to use.

- ◆ 'I research extensively – more than I will ever need – because everything I read feeds my ideas for plot development and incident, especially incident.' (Joan Hessayon)

Some details will have to be checked as you come across the need for them while you write. During later revision you may need to check or confirm facts.

Note the sources of facts you collect, in case you need to go back for more details, or have to provide proof.

Action points

Make lists, with addresses and telephone numbers, of:

1. Libraries in your area, particularly big or special ones, with, if possible, names of contacts – people you know or have met or spoken to during earlier research. It is easier to ask for a specific person, and makes a good impression that you remember them.

2. Museums and theme parks in your area.

3. People you know or have been told about who have any expert knowledge. Most experts are only too happy to answer questions or talk about their speciality.

4. Internet sites you find useful, and may want to return to. It's advisable to note the topic, since the names or addresses (URLs) of these sites do not always indicate what they display.

Being methodical

Arrange your notes for easy reference. Use folders, record cards, or computer files, whichever is most convenient.

DISCUSSION POINTS

1. Write down as many themes as you can think of, and under each one make notes of the sort of plots they inspire.

2. Write down a detailed list of everything you did today, read, heard on radio, watched on TV, and the people you saw. Try to find an idea from each item or person which might become an incident in a novel.

3. Think of some different settings, such as Roman Britain, present-day Australia, an oil company, a spaceship voyage, and make lists of the sort of research you might have to do for each and how you would set about it.

$$\text{3}$$

Creating the Right Characters

CHOOSING YOUR CAST WITH CARE

I use the word 'cast' deliberately, since your characters are actors in a drama. See them this way, in scenes on a stage. It helps to bring them alive for you, and therefore helps you to make them real for your readers. Visualise the action as it takes place. Most writers find this works.

- ◆ 'I find it very useful (particularly in thrillers or action stories) to draft in dialogue only, no descriptions, no scene-setting. Once the words are there, it's much easier to see where the exposition should be.' (Frederick Nolan)

Characters must be right for your novel. They can provide ideas for the plot, for incidents and twists.

- ◆ 'The action arises from the people in the story reacting in character to the situation in which they find themselves.' (Ann Hulme)

Deciding how many characters

Create as few as you can get away with. P. G. Wodehouse said one big one was worth two small ones. There will be:

(a) Some who are essential in order to do certain things; these vary from the main characters to the unseen train driver without whom they could not move around.

(b) Real people have family, friends, neighbours and colleagues. They give your main characters a background with all the relationships and complications involved, even if they don't feature directly in the story.

(c) Others round out the lives or demonstrate character traits of the main characters, even if off-stage. This could be a bedridden old lady the heroine visits, which can show her compassion or helpfulness.

Making them know their places

The scale of importance varies. In category romances very few characters appear apart from the hero and heroine. In most crime novels several characters have to be of similar importance to provide a believable list of suspects.

Checklist

On your list you are likely to have:

- Two at the top: the hero and heroine, the sleuths, the opposing army commanders. These are the main **protagonists**.

- In some types of plots, crime or science fiction or thrillers, there may be an **antagonist** against whom the protagonist must battle.

- Perhaps several biggish ones who are on stage a lot, powerful enough to influence events and about whom readers *care*. Caring is not liking. Readers care about a character when they want him to receive his just deserts, be this reward or punishment. If readers are indifferent to a **major character** the writer has not succeeded.

♦ Some **minor characters** who play important parts, but don't appear very much.

♦ And the **walk-ons** like waiters and postmen who are essential in the tasks they perform, but only scenery.

Action points
Get organised:

1. Take a novel you know well and list all the characters in order of importance, labelled protagonists, antagonist (if there is one), major, minor and walk-ons. Could any of them be dispensed with totally, or their role be given to another character?

2. Do the same with your own casts of characters.

FLESHING OUT CHARACTERS

Having a variety
In most plots you need people of different sexes, ages, appearances, occupations and dispositions. This makes the situation more natural and interesting.

♦ 'Ideally every character should have an individual voice (as people do in life) – particular turns of speech, favourite phrases, a tendency to be slangy or pedantic.' (Reay Tannahill)

Readers often like to read about people from similar groups to their own, but they also want characters to be intriguing, different from themselves.

In certain stories characters need someone in whom they can confide or with whom they can discuss or share information. Most detectives have a sidekick, most heroines a best friend. Make these characters interesting in themselves, active in the story. Give them other functions. Maybe a sub-plot revolves round them.

Getting to know them

Many writers, though not all, compile lists of their characters' physical and other attributes before they start.

♦ 'Write a potted biography for each one.' (Andrew Puckett)

This helps writers to remember what characters look like, but also to know how they might react to various situations. They are notes for guidance, however, and are not necessarily used in the book. As the book progresses, too, other attributes are likely to be added to the basic list.

Checklist: building a character profile

Answer these twenty questions about your main protagonists and major characters. Can you think of other questions?

♦ name
♦ age and date of birth

Two examples of different characters – Plot out of characters

	Kate	Ann
Name	Kate	Ann
Age	25	21
Physical appearance	tall, slim, strong features, long red hair, green eyes	medium height, short wavy brown hair, brown eyes, slightly plump, pretty
Occupation	freelance artist	secretary to sales manager of local factory
Family background	Father a diplomat, retired; mother remarried to a French count ten years ago; older brother, policeman	Father a bank manager; mother dead five years ago; younger sister, 16, at school
Schooling	expelled from three boarding schools	local comprehensive, top of class, prefect
Disposition	extrovert	confident but quiet and dreamy
Where lives now	flat in London	home, country town
With whom	two girls and two men sharing	father and sister
Clothes liked	offbeat, latest fashion	good classics, has a few disasters with experiments
Hobbies/interests/ likes/dislikes	powerful motorbike; travel to exotic places; likes jazz, indifferent to food, hates cats	cooking, music, environmental and 'green' issues; enjoys foreign foods, country and western, dislikes arguments
Virtues	casually kind, fierce against injustice	well organised, competent, soft-hearted
Faults	always short of cash, quick-tempered	critical of sister, obstinate
Previous romantic history	two lovers, brief affairs which she ended	engaged at 19 to salesman at work, he jilted her for her best friend

Fig. 1. Two character profiles.

- physical appearance
- family background
- where brought up
- schooling
- where lives now
- with whom
- first job
- other jobs
- present occupation
- disposition
- clothes liked/disliked
- hobbies/interests
- other likes/dislikes (*eg* food, music, books, animals)
- virtues
- faults
- ambitions
- secrets
- romantic history.

Action points: characters and plots

1. Keep this outline ready and refer to it when you are creating new characters.

2. Look at the diagram in Figure 1 listing the characteristics of two different girls, and try to see what kinds of conflicts might develop, what plots might be possible using them.

Names are critical

Names do far more than identify characters. Some authors cannot begin until they have named their cast. Names can tell you a lot.

- Family names can indicate social inheritance (Saddler or Fitzroy) or ethnic background (O'Leary or Patel).

- First names often indicate age if associated with film stars (Marilyn or Wayne) or an event or passing fashion (Jubilee or the Puritan names such as Temperance).

- Characters may be named after a relative or historical personage, which can say something about their parents, as do names which are either very popular or unusual.

- Hard sounds indicate curtness, soft ones gentleness.

- Make sure your characters are easily differentiated by having some names short, some long, and of different rhythms or patterns, such as the stress on first or last syllable.

- Don't have the same initial letter for similar characters unless it's important to the plot.

- If your story takes place in a real town, now or in the past, with a solicitor called Harvey Anstruther, make sure there isn't such a real person. Check telephone, commercial, street and professional directories.

- Characters may be called something different by other characters. Mr Brown can be David, darling, daddy, grandpa, sir, or you bastard. The narrator should always refer to him by the same name, introduce him by that one, and make it obvious who is calling him by what variation.

Make lists of names, and the characteristics you might associate with each. Then ask deeper questions, give the characters a twist, and find less obvious attributes.

Action points: keeping track

There are many ways to help you remember your characters, apart from the profile you have compiled.

1. Cut photographs from magazines and newspapers of people who resemble your characters, and keep them visible.

2. List the main physical and other details alongside for reference. If you have room put the profiles there too.

3. Draw up family trees with dates of birth, marriage and death.

4. Draw diagrams of their houses and neighbourhoods, decorate and people them.

5. Avoid the trap of putting all this into your novel. Like most other research it's for guidance, helps you to be accurate, propping up what's visible but not intruding. Only mention a fact when it's relevant.

6. Keep away from stereotypes, apart from walk-ons who don't want to be noticeable by having any peculiarity.

7. Make your characters complex, with many different facets while still being recognisable. You could exaggerate something, or give them an obsession, to make them more interesting.

8. If a character is going to behave in an especially odd manner, though, give clues early on, don't spring it on the unsuspecting reader.

9. Start collecting a rogues' gallery of photos to use in the future.

Believing in your characters

They must be absolutely real to you, or you won't make readers believe in them. Live with them, get inside them, know them as well as you possibly can. We all give something of ourselves when we write fiction, and though we might never commit murder we have to be able to know what it feels like to want to do it. We are complex people with good and bad points, our characters must be too.

Creating sympathy for them

A character is 'sympathetic' when the reader believes in him, likes him, can imagine being him, approves his aims, wants him to achieve them. Readers approve of protagonists who are admirable, dependable, generous. They loathe bullying or ruthless greed, though they may be fascinated by such characters and enjoy the *frisson* of meeting them.

◆ 'You have to start with a personality that attracts. The reader has to identify. Heroes can't be wimpish.' (Joan Hessayon)

◆ 'Make your main characters your friends – if you love them there is more chance of your readers doing the same.' (Anita Burgh)

If your protagonist has only unpleasant or despicable traits most readers won't identify with him, although they might understand him. If a protagonist is a victim he must still be strong, it shouldn't be his own fault, and he mustn't give up. His sacrifices must be worth while.

I asked some not-yet-published novelists what they found most difficult. 'Characterisation' (Diana Atkinson) was a typical reply. It must be worked on.

Agents and editors look for:

- ◆ 'Characters.' (Caroline Sheldon)
- ◆ 'Good characters.' (Jane Morpeth)
- ◆ 'Good characterisation.' (Bob Tanner)
- ◆ 'Carefully developed characters.' (Laura Longrigg)
- ◆ 'Involvement with the characters.' (Elizabeth Johnson)
- ◆ 'Getting involved with the characters, caring about them.' (Dorothy Lumley)
- ◆ 'Original characters.' (Beverley Cousins)
- ◆ 'Being interested in the characters, caring what happens to them, and how.' (Deborah Smith)
- ◆ 'Good characterisation.' (Barbara Boote).

Readers want:

- ◆ 'I must care about the characters.' (Judy Phillips)
- ◆ 'Interesting and believable characters.' (Joan Beard)
- ◆ 'Some depth to characters.' (Valerie Bennett).

Making your characters grow
Many changes occur as time passes, marriage and

children, different houses and jobs, but we also change in response to experiences. Your characters must too. They must be different at the end of the story, because of the conflict and its resolution, and this difference can be an improvement or not. It must be believable, however. Often the apparent change is in effect a discovery, a stripping away of a surface disguise to the real character beneath.

Showing your characters

You need to transfer your character profiles into your novel without being obvious. You cannot simply list the character's qualities in a piece of description. This would be boring, difficult for the reader to absorb, and unsubtle. In the same way as you know real people from what they are and do, you can portray your characters indirectly.

Checklist

Show characters by:

- what they do now
- what they have done in the past
- how they do things
- why they do things
- how other people see them
- how other people talk about them
- how other people behave towards them
- their beliefs, habits, hobbies, interests, tastes, preferences
- what they say and how they say it.

Letting characters take over

Cardboard, two-dimensional characters are puppets which the author pushes around. If you have created truly believable people you may find that your plans for them aren't compatible with how they are. Then you need to adjust either the character or the plot. One story may work with a certain character, not with others. Authors who create characters and follow where they lead know this, and their books don't depend a great deal on plot. Authors who rely too much on a pre-ordained plot may find their characters wooden and incredible. Most novels are a balance.

◆ 'I have to be sure that both plot and characters will be strong enough to stand up to what I want of them, and it's surprising how many apparently promising ideas turn out to be far too slight.' (Reay Tannahill)

Action point
Look at some books you've read recently. Which are character-led, which plot-led, which balanced? Add these to your card or computer index.

WORKING OUT RELATIONSHIPS AND CONFLICTS

Keeping the heroes on-stage
The protagonists, the most important characters, should be on stage as often as possible.

◆ They should be given most to do, should be active and make things happen, not simply react to events.

◆ They must solve the mystery, tackle the villain, perform the heroic tasks.

◆ They should not be there performing a minor role while a subsidiary character takes the limelight or does something heroic which your main character could have done.

- Their aims must be laudable.

- They must face and overcome difficulties.

- They must be strong though vulnerable.

- Some imperfections can be attractive, and even murder by a hero could be acceptable in a good cause, such as destroying a terrorist.

- 'One hundred per cent nice characters are very difficult to bring to life. Even the most romantic heroes and heroines need a few human failings.' (Reay Tannahill)

Provide conflict

Whatever the cause of conflict, readers must care about the result. What's at stake has to be important, to matter greatly. The protagonists or opposing sides have different aims which cannot both be achieved, although the reader may want both to be achieved. Then a satisfactory solution or compromise has to be found. There can also be inner conflict when one character has contradictory objectives.

Action point

Make a list of as many causes of conflict as you can think of, from books you have read or your imagination.

DISCUSSION POINTS

1. If you have decided what sort of novel to write, make a list of possible characters and how you might use them.

2. Take a well-known fictional character like Jane Eyre or Oliver Twist, put them in a new age and place and

situation, and work out how they might behave and with what consequences. What effects might a different historical and social background have on their characters?

3. Take three characters, let's say a wimpish young man, a bossy young woman, and a middle-aged mother of three boys. They see a nasty fight begin between two young teenage lads, and one boy pulls a knife. How would each react? Write the scene showing what they might do and say.

4

Getting Ready to Start

You have an idea, a plot and some characters. You will have lots of notes, and maybe a rough outline of what you mean to do. There are several more decisions to make before you can begin to set the novel down in narrative form.

CHOOSING THE RIGHT TITLE

This doesn't have to be chosen first, but titles often come during the planning stage. Consider ideas now, since a title often expresses the main theme of the novel.

Sometimes titles only come when the book is finished. A phrase, or incident, or character can give an idea. Don't worry if you can't think of the ideal title now, but work hard to find a good one before you send your manuscript out.

Titles are important

Some editors say a good title helps catch their attention.

- 'A good title is one of the most important parts of a novel.' (Luigi Bonomi)

A sparkling or intriguing title helps to sell a book, according to booksellers. Agents were not so positive, but at this stage titles can be changed, and frequently are. Publishers may have their own preferences, or they may have published a book with a similar title and don't want to confuse readers. Librarians were divided about whether titles attracted readers, and most readers said they went mainly for familiar authors rather than titles, though titles might put them off reading a book.

- ◆ 'I think I could be discouraged.' (Hanna Bridgeman)
- ◆ 'Can be off-putting.' (Ruislip Literary Society)

Although titles appear less significant to readers, they still matter.

Readers only see what has been published. Your first readers are agents and editors, who will see your originality and writing talent.

Titles must be appropriate

Ideally titles are short, two or three words, since these fit better onto a book jacket and spine. Words of two and three syllables, with a rhythm, work best.

They should convey something about the *type* of book. Look at how many crime books use the words murder, death, or mystery; and romances love, bride, or heart. Historicals try to indicate the period, and recent blockbusters have used the themes as one-word titles.

Finding titles

Many titles are straightforward descriptions, while others come from puns, or plays on words or common phrases.

Some use alliteration. Many are quotations or phrases from poems, Shakespeare or the Bible.

Keep in mind your intended reader and choose something which they will understand and appreciate.

Action points: finding titles

1. Think up some alternative titles for famous books, or ones you have read recently.

2. Make lists of titles you might one day use.

USING THE RIGHT VIEWPOINTS

The choice you make now will have important implications for how you tell the story.

Choosing the most effective viewpoint

Viewpoint is the manner in which the story is told, through whose eyes. It's as if the scene is being told by one of the characters. When you are reading a book notice how an author keeps the main interest of a scene or chapter with one person, and shows as if from inside her how she feels, and how she sees the actions and emotions of others.

Different stories require different approaches, and no one method is best for every story or every author. Decide which characters, one or more, can best tell the story.

There are technical terms describing the options, such as **omniscient**. This means that the narrator sees everything from some lofty outside standpoint, entering into each character's mind in turn, but having an overall view separate from them all. Many Victorian novels were written like this. It keeps the reader at a distance from the characters, not allowing them to identify with any one for very long, and is little used today.

There are two main viewpoint techniques used today, **first** or **third** person, and both usually told in **past tense**.

First person problems

The first person (I) narrator, where one character tells the story as if she is writing it, is sometimes essential, and often used. It can be effective in conveying intense emotion, or in a crime novel, where readers have only the same information as the narrator, usually the sleuth. However, there can be difficulties.

- You need devices to have her present when important things happen, or being told of them in an interesting way. She needs valid reasons for obtaining the information.

- If this means eavesdropping or reading letters it can reflect badly on the protagonist.

- The fact that she is telling the story means she survived threats or danger, so an element of suspense is lost.

- She can only tell what she sees and interprets of other people's actions, feelings and emotions, or what they tell her, and this may not be the full truth.

- It is sometimes difficult to avoid the impression of being self-absorbed, with too many 'I's, or boring or boastful, especially if the narrator is the heroine and has to describe her own brave or meritorious actions.

Third person techniques

A third person narrator can tell the story mainly through one person's eyes.

- This will tend to be male or female depending on the likely readership.

- It will usually be the main protagonist.

- The author can switch viewpoint to other characters, for example in scenes when the main character is absent, or get inside other characters and show their emotions.

- It is the most used today, it's the simplest method and usually best to begin with, until you have more experience.

How many viewpoints?

If you choose the third person viewpoint you can use it in various ways, but bear the following points in mind.

- Keep the viewpoint characters to a minimum, because switching demands special skills, and too many viewpoints can be confusing and diffuse attention and sympathy.

- Normally use the main characters, though it can be effective, very occasionally, to show a scene through the eyes of a character uninvolved in that specific conflict.

- It's best, at least to start with, to keep to the same viewpoint within one chapter.

- In long chapters broken up into several distinct scenes

keep one viewpoint per scene. Switching too frequently confuses the readers.

◆ Use a pattern. For example, don't have a single viewpoint for half the novel, and then start switching every scene. It confuses the reader's expectations.

Action points: looking at viewpoints

1. Read a book written from the first person viewpoint, and see where the author has constructed devices such as a letter, or eavesdropping, or a report from someone else to allow the narrator access to information.

2. Read another book where several third person viewpoints are used, and make a list of who narrates, and when the changes are made. Is a pattern emerging?

ESTABLISHING YOUR VOICE

Our physical speaking voices differ from those of others. We write more formally than we talk, choosing different words and sentence constructions. We use gestures when talking, and other aids like punctuation when writing. We both talk and write differently depending on our audience. When talking, if we are astute we detect lack of comprehension in our audience and adjust what we say accordingly. We cannot do this when writing so have to be aware of likely problems and forestall them.

All these different ways of communicating are our own very special styles, using our individual voice. Experts can often identify an author or composer from a small fragment of writing or musical score.

Voices with special qualities of freshness, humour, clarity or perceptiveness will be recognised and valued.

Don't attempt to copy anyone else's style. You won't do it consistently or with conviction, and falsity seems to be magnified and becomes glaringly out of place.

GETTING THE BEGINNING RIGHT

Now you can start writing the first chapter, which is perhaps the most important one you have to do. The first few sentences can make or break a novel.

The narrative hook

A title and **jacket**, which most librarians thought very important, may tempt readers to pick your book from the shelves. Jackets often indicate the type of book, with bright or dark colours, blood, guns and daggers, abstract designs, pastoral scenes, sassy looking or shawl-wrapped girls. One librarian said a bad cover design wouldn't prevent a reader taking a book by an author she knew, and in any case most books were displayed with only the spine showing. However, a librarian pointed out: 'Attractive artwork will encourage us to use it in displays.'

And books displayed, as well as those on the returns trolley, are often the first chosen by many readers.

Potential readers may look at the **blurb**, which both readers and librarians rated as more important than the title, but in most cases they then turn to page one. This is where you must tempt readers to continue and not replace the book on the shelf. You need to work especially hard to get the first few paragraphs as perfect as possible.

Publishers almost always control the jacket, and though authors may be consulted they don't have the final say. But the author does have control over the opening paragraphs.

Action point

Read these two openings, and say which you prefer and why. Which would you be most likely to read further?

Evergreen

Angela Jones sighed as she looked out of the staffroom window. It was raining cats and dogs, and she'd forgotten her umbrella again. She would be drenched when she reached home, for it was a good half-hour's walk.

Angela's home was a small terraced house in Pitsfield, a suburb of Shelcaster. It had once been a mining village, and her father still worked in the last remaining coalmine in the area. His father and grandfather had also worked there, as had her mother's father and brothers.

Her parents had been determined to let Angela take every chance that came her way, and had denied themselves small luxuries so that she could stay on at school to take her A-levels, and then go to the local university. It would have been too expensive for her to go anywhere else, they'd said, and besides, they wanted their ewe-lamb to stay at home with them.

So Angela had worked hard, taken a lower second in English, and done her teacher training. She'd been fortunate to find a job in Lodge Road First School, so near to home, but so far when it was raining and there were no buses going cross-country.

> ### The Tinderbox
>
> Annie swore vividly as she stepped into a deep puddle. And to think that only a week ago she'd been praying for rain. Things changed! She leaned forward to look at the muddy splashes on her new tights, then gasped as her elbows were seized by hard, relentless fingers.
>
> 'You're a menace even without an umbrella!' a deep masculine voice said angrily.
>
> Annie struggled to free herself and her purse slipped from under her arm. 'You! Now look what you've done. What on earth are you doing here anyway? I thought you'd gone to Syria. And let me go, you're hurting.'
>
> She struggled, but was dragged ruthlessly into the shelter of a doorway. Her umbrella was taken from her hands, shaken viciously then furled, and a moment later her purse, streaming muddy water, was thrust at her. 'You told Sara we were going to be married. Why?'
>
> Annie took a deep breath. 'I – I – well, I meant it for the best,' she eventually stammered. 'I thought it was a good idea.'
>
> He laughed, unamused. 'You've never had a good idea in your life. You're a walking disaster zone, and I'm going to make damned sure you never again interfere in my life!'

Comparison of the sample openings

Titles

1. *Evergreen* sounds dull and old-fashioned.

2. *The Tinderbox* gives more indication of excitement.

Action

1. Almost none, just description and thoughts.

2. Immediate physical and verbal conflict.

Style

1. Many clichés (raining cats and dogs, take every chance that came her way, denied themselves small luxuries, ewe-lamb), the language is gentle, and only the first paragraph is from Angela's viewpoint. The rest is exposition.

2. From Annie's viewpoint, and contains expressive words.

Character

1. Angela is dependent on her family, not very clever if she only obtained a lower-second degree after working hard, and somewhat complaining as she sighs about the rain.

2. Annie has strong emotions, can perhaps laugh at herself (Things changed!), gets into scrapes, and doesn't think ahead. Which girl is the more interesting?

Future promise

1. Almost no questions to ask about Angela. No idea what sort of story it might be. No conflict looming.

2. With Annie, though, we want to know who the man is, why she thought he was in Syria, who Sara is, and why Annie told her she was getting married when she wasn't, and how he is going to stop her from further

interference. There's plenty of conflict promised.

Making it active

The most effective beginning is to get right into the action. You can begin with a description of a setting or a character, but this is static, less easy to do, and can therefore be boring. It's not advisable until you have acquired a lot of skill.

Action implies a scene, with characters. They are doing something, preferably caught in the middle, bang, not about to begin with a lot of build-up and explanation. If possible make it just before a major event or confrontation. You can give the necessary background information later on, explain who they are and what is happening. If you have enticed readers to turn over the first page in order to find this out you are half-way to persuading them to read the whole book. And always remember that your first reader is the editor who may buy your book.

Readers' views

Readers said it was important that books:

- 'gain my interest in the first few pages.' (Jo Crocker)

- have 'good style and story.' (Sylvia Parker)

- have a 'style of writing which you know from the first page – the book grabs you or not.' (Molly Frearson)

- and, when choosing 'I look at the first part.' (Jill Rundle)

- 'I like to get into it quickly.' (Judy Phillips)

Agents said the same. Scripts stood out with:

- 'the ability to tell a story which hooks the reader from the first page.' (Sarah Molloy)

- and 'an urge to read on after the first few pages.' (Bob Tanner)

Editors tell the same story:

- 'a powerful opening chapter.' (Luigi Bonomi)

Checklist

The functions of the first few pages are:

- to attract the reader's interest
- to indicate the type of book
- to show the mood and style of the writing
- to introduce the main character, and perhaps one or two others
- to engage the reader's sympathy for one of the characters, make them care what happens
- to establish the time and place
- to make the reader feel that something good is coming.

Preparing for what follows

If you start with a dramatic event, make sure you can follow it with something better. If it's the most dramatic event in the story the rest is a let-down. Novels need variations, ups and downs in the level of intensity, but the main crisis should be as near the end as possible.

Don't confuse the readers

If you are introduced to a dozen strangers at once, can you remember all their names? Don't bring in too many characters to begin with, or the reader will be confused. They need time to absorb what to them is new information.

It isn't necessary to explain everything at the start. If you pose sufficiently intriguing questions the reader will want to continue in order to find the answers.

Coming back to it

If your beginning isn't right, don't get bogged down. A frequent reason for not completing a novel is that the would-be writer spends all his time perfecting the beginning, and never gets past chapter one.

Carry on, write the rest of the book, and come back to the beginning later. Many authors do it last of all, since a later incident can often suggest the ideal opening. And you may find that information you tried to include in the first few pages fits more naturally later on.

Action point

Practise writing good openings. It doesn't have to be a real novel you are working on, but develop ideas as they come, and file them for future possible use.

DISCUSSION POINTS

1. Take a dozen titles and see if you can discover where the authors found them. Are they appropriate, and what do they say about the contents, type or style of the books?

2. Look really closely at several novels. Can you find anything distinctive about the writing, the treatment of characters, ways of expressing things, humour, or imagery which gives the writers a special or unusual 'voice'?

3. Look at the checklist on the functions of the first page. Apply these to several novels, some you have read and some new to you, chosen at random. How far have the writers succeeded in doing everything? If they haven't in some cases, can you suggest reasons?

⑤

Looks and Language

PRESENTATION MATTERS

Your manuscript will not yet be ready for submission, but start to set your work out in the conventional manner so that it becomes normal to you. It will save time later.

First impressions

We are tempted to judge people on first impressions. They may be wrong, but it is difficult to overcome them. To give your manuscript the maximum chance of success, an agent's or an editor's first impression of it must be favourable. Their offices are very busy, they have many submissions, and may be able to spare very little time for each. Anything which looks scruffy or difficult or unprofessional could well be sent straight back unread.

Every agent and editor said that the presentation of a manuscript was important.

- 'It needs to be clean, double spacing, one side of the page and *not* heavily edited in pen by the side.' (Judy Piatkus)

- 'A well produced typescript suggests that the author cares about his/her work and is at least trying to be professional.' (Michael Legat)

♦ 'If it appears that an author does not care about their manuscript, then why should an editor? I have been severely put off novels that are littered with spelling mistakes or scribbles.' (Luigi Bonomi)

♦ 'Over-immaculate presentation – thick, quality paper, borders, artwork, fancy fonts – looks pretentious.' (Margaret James)

Make it as clean, neat and professional as possible. It is counter-productive to devise elaborate covering sheets, provide pictures of possible covers, or huge-lettered title pages in an attempt to make it look like a real book. This shrieks of the amateur who is afraid his manuscript will not be good enough on its own and needs props. The props hinder rather than help.

The conventional layout

Most publishers will ask for a copy on computer disk ready for publication, but don't send one first unless they specifically ask for it this way. Very few publishers will accept them. If you are considering electronic publishing on the Internet, also check requirements. They vary. Some publishers want hard copy (a paper manuscript) as well as a disk. Maybe when electronic readers are widely available, and have a common format, this will change, but at the moment it doesn't always apply. There are several reasons for this:

♦ The disk may not be compatible with the publisher's system.

♦ Editors do not have time in the office to read

submissions, sitting before a screen. They read in taxis, on buses and trains, at home, in the bath. They need hard copy for convenience, and won't print out your disk to get it.

◆ I dislike scripts 'submitted on disk without a hard copy.' (Barbara Boote)

A manuscript must be typed, or word processed, using an average size ten letters to the inch type, in a clear **font**, one which isn't so fancy it's difficult to read. Use the same font and size throughout. Lasers and inkjet printers are the best, and lasers are usually cheaper to run, but if you have a dot-matrix printer or typewriter use a black ribbon, and when it fades renew it. Don't use the draft mode which tends to be very faint.

The lines should be double spaced, and with wide (2–3cm) margins all round. This allows future editorial changes to be written in, or instructions to the typesetter.

With these margins you will normally have twenty-eight to thirty lines per page, between ten and twelve words per line. Use A4-sized white paper, preferably 80 gram weight so that the page beneath doesn't show through.

Pages should be numbered consecutively throughout, not starting each new chapter with page one.

Checklist
You need a title page with:

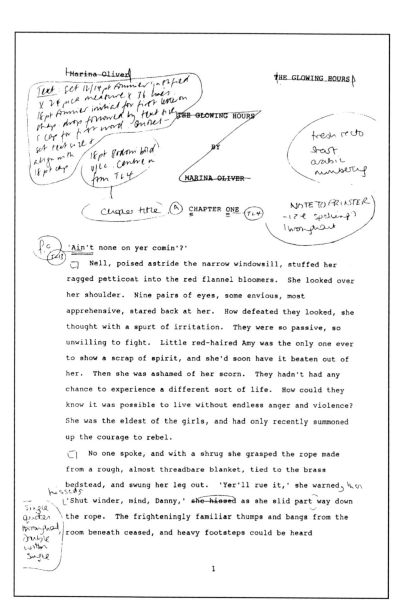

Fig. 2. An edited page of a script.

- your name and address and a daytime telephone number, fax and email if you have them
- pseudonym if you are using one
- the book's title
- the approximate number of words.

Also:

- put your address on the final page too
- you can put your name and title at the top or bottom of each page, but make it clear this is not part of the text by having a line or a space between it and the text.

Pseudonyms

People use **pseudonyms** for many reasons. Their own name might be too difficult, not sound right, they prefer anonymity, or write more than one type of book.

Counting words

With computers it is possible to count the precise numbers of words, and more publishers now accept this method, but this can be misleading. A book with lots of short dialogue and many chapters will occupy more space than one with little dialogue and a few long chapters. It's the total pages the book will have that interests a publisher, so that he can work out printing and type-setting costs.

To calculate total **wordage** take the average number of words in ten complete lines, say 12, multiply by the number of lines in a complete page, say 30, then by the total number of manuscript pages, 300. 12 x 30 x 300 = 108,000 words. 'Approx 110,000 words' on your title page is enough.

Marina Oliver

The Laurels

High Town

Midshire

Tel: 019 876 5432

Email: marina@the laurels.com

A CLANDESTINE AFFAIR

by

SALLY JAMES
(Pseudonym of MARINA OLIVER)

Approx 60,000 words

Fig. 3. A title page.

Action point
Check several of your own pages, properly laid out as in Figure 5, and find out your average number of words per page.

Page layout
Indent all paragraphs, apart from the first ones in the chapter and after a break, which in a printed book will be indicated by a space. You can show a break by some mark such as * * *. The indentation should be big enough to make it perfectly clear it is a new paragraph; the first pre-set tab of half an inch or one centimetre is usual.

Don't, as in non-indented business correspondence, leave extra spaces between paragraphs.

In dialogue each new speaker must have a new paragraph, indented. You can put the spoken words after some introduction, without starting a new paragraph, if the introduction leads up to the speech. For example:

John looked at her and sighed. 'Come here,' he said.

Publishers have house styles for details such as single or double inverted commas, so unless you know which publisher you are writing for you can't know which to use. Just be consistent.

Helping the editor
You want to make it easy for editors to handle your work, as well as making it look professional.

Checklist: sending a manuscript

♦ Never pin or fasten pages together. Stabbed, bleeding editors are not receptive ones.

♦ Don't put pages in a ring binder. Editors tend to read on trains or at home, where a heavy manuscript which can't be split up into convenient sections is a nuisance.

♦ A rubber band or envelope folder is enough to keep pages together and tidy.

♦ Send the manuscript in a strong padded envelope. Ordinary envelopes tend to split if the parcel is heavy.

♦ Don't use lots of string, fancy knots, or lashings of sticky tape. By the time editors have fought their way in they aren't in the mood for kind judgements.

♦ Include a simple covering letter and return postage. Editors and agents are sensitive too. They could throw away submissions without return postage, or 'otherwise the agent or publisher has to ask for it, which is embarrassing.' (Laura Longrigg)

♦ A big, self-stick, self-addressed return label is easier than including another padded envelope.

♦ Always keep a copy of what you have sent. It doesn't happen often, but manuscripts can be lost.

MAKING LANGUAGE WORK FOR YOU

The way a writer uses vocabulary, sentence structure and imagery is part of her style. Aim for clarity, conciseness, precision and simplicity. Vary sentence and paragraph length and avoid a monotonous rhythm or construction. Good writing is clear and easy to understand. Beginners

THE WRONG LAYOUT

'You can't expect me to swing that heavy handle,' Kitty said disbelievingly.

'Darling, be sensible! It's the only way to start the motor,' Timothy replied.

'But it's heavy!' 'Not as bad as you imagine. Come on, try it.'

'I have my new dress on.'

'And when you go driving you'll always have good clothes on. You can keep it out of the way.'

Reluctantly Kitty climbed down from the driving seat and took the starting handle in a fastidious grasp.

Fig. 4. An example of poor layout.

THE RIGHT LAYOUT

'You can't expect me to swing that heavy handle,' Kitty said disbelievingly.
'Darling, be sensible! It's the only way to start the motor,' Timothy replied.
'But it's heavy!'
'Not as bad as you imagine. Come on, try it.'
'I have my new dress on.'
'And when you go driving you'll always have good clothes on. You can keep it out of the way.'
Reluctantly Kitty climbed down from the driving seat and took the starting handle in a fastidious grasp.

Fig. 5. An example of good layout.
From *The Glowing Hours* by Marina Oliver.

allow language to become extravagant in the mistaken belief that this is 'literary'. They use too many adjectives and adverbs, produce over-elaborate descriptions, and concentrate on finding esoteric words instead of the most appropriate. They litter their work with strained imagery and obscure allusions. This is overwriting.

Using language effectively

These writers have forgotten they are in the business of communication. If we want our work to be read with appreciation and understood correctly we need to use language as effectively as possible.

Agents reject:

* 'poor writing' (Sarah Molloy)
* 'bad English...overwritten situations, too many adjectives.' (Bob Tanner)

Editors appreciate:

* 'tight writing' (Beverley Cousins)
* 'a powerful writing style.' (Luigi Bonomi)

USING GRAMMAR, PUNCTUATION AND SPELLING

Tools to make our work easier

Some schoolteachers and creative writing tutors maintain that what is said is more important than the manner of its saying. They extol imagination, creativity and self-expression, and condemn any attempts to impose what they despise as 'restrictive rules and conventions' on this undisciplined outpouring.

They've missed the point.

Grammar and punctuation and spelling are not pedantic requirements which can safely be ignored. They are tools which help us to convey our thoughts accurately and unambiguously. We are speaking the same language as our listeners, and helping them to understand what we say with greater ease and fewer distractions. Anything which causes the reader to pause, try to work out what was meant, or go back and see whether that really was what the writer intended to say, is poor communication.

- 'I ... always like an author who uses words well and understands grammar and punctuation and can spell.' (Michael Legat)

- A pet hate is 'bad spelling.' (Barbara Boote).

These days there are spellcheckers on most word processing packages, and tricks such as underlining or highlighting mistakes. But beware! Often these come with American spellings, or cannot cope with the various endings, or proper names. They are useful for pointing out typing errors, but don't rely on them exclusively. Most of us have quirks, words we are always unsure of. You can usually add these to a personal spellchecker.

A practical consideration
Editors faced with two novels of equal interest, but room in their list for one, will choose the one which gives them less work correcting grammatical and other mistakes.

Action points: books to get

1. You probably already have a dictionary. A spelling dictionary, or a specialised writer's dictionary, as well as a dictionary of synonyms would also be useful.

2. If you are in the least unsure of grammatical rules and punctuation conventions, get a simple grammar book. Several are recommended in the reading list at the end of this book.

A reviewer commented: 'Often a less accomplished writer has grammatical tics which show up promiscuously – in the dialogue of many different characters as well as in the narrative.' Watch out for your own.

There are Internet sites with a thesaurus or dictionary online, sites about grammar which explain punctuation and other 'rules', and where you can even ask questions. You can get help on style from newsgroups, though the people answering may not be experts, so you need to judge their advice carefully.

USING VOCABULARY, SLANG AND DIALECT

Choosing the most effective words

Aim for brevity and lucidity. A strong verb is better than a qualifying adverb. 'He strolled' is more vivid than 'he walked slowly'. An exact noun is better than a dozen adjectives. 'Iceberg' is better than 'a large, floating lump of frozen seawater'.

Of course this does not mean you can never use adverbs and adjectives, but use them sparingly, and when you are revising make sure each one is necessary. Watch for the phrases that are so common they have become clichés – like 'bouncing baby' or 'brakes squealing'.

Being wary of modifiers

When an adverb or adjective comes before the verb or noun it is **modifying**, particularly if there are several intervening words, it is weak, since we don't yet know what it is modifying. Words like rather, quite, a little, also weaken the effect. 'She was rather beautiful', and 'he was quite angry' are not very forceful or interesting comments.

Being positive

Show characters experiencing the external world and use specific examples instead of generalisations. Instead of 'it was very windy', you can convey the information more vividly if you have the wind blow a leaf into a character's face. Avoid passive verbs and tenses. 'He watched' is more forceful than 'he was watching'. 'He frowned' is better than 'he looked annoyed'. 'The dog barked' is more direct than 'there was a sound of a dog barking'.

Slang gets dated

Unless you want to illustrate that your novel takes place in a particular time or section of society, avoid slang. Even a couple of years later it can sound very odd, and what was current when you wrote your novel could be out of date by the time the book is in the shops.

◆ (I don't like) 'too much slang.' (Bob Tanner)

It has become fashionable with some kinds of books to use profanities and obscenities very freely. Authors may feel they are being realistic or liberated, but even these words have to be used by the appropriate characters – not everyone uses them or likes them.

♦ (I don't like) 'swear words.' (Barbara Boote)

Pronunciation and dialect

It's always difficult to decide whether to portray regional, or foreign or uneducated speech with phonetic spelling, and apostrophes indicating missing letters. Reading pages and pages of such speech can be very irritating, and it's better to hint at it than try to reproduce it accurately.

A similar problem occurs with dialect and foreign words. Too many hide the meaning from readers unfamiliar with them. A few words, intelligible from the context, are enough to give the flavour of the region or person.

♦ One reviewer disliked 'epigrams in foreign, untranslated, languages.'

However, if you need to have a character say a few words in his own language, even one you don't know, you can buy simple translation programs for your computer. Even so, it's always wise to try to find someone who does speak the language to check this, if you can.

With historicals you need to avoid modern terms, but also too many archaic ones like prithee and forsooth.

In all three situations turns of phrase, changing the order of words in a sentence, or different patterns and rhythms of speech can do the job more effectively.

USING DIALOGUE

Novels need dialogue. You have to solve an apparent contradiction. It is not ordinary speech with hesitations, repetitions, pauses, interruptions in trains of thought and confused explanations, but it must sound natural. Omit irrelevant chit-chat, and lengthy discussions or arrangements concerning actions which will be shown later.

◆ 'Ordinary speech copied straight onto the page will sound, as anyone who has read a transcript of a live broadcast will confirm, ungrammatical and barely literate.' (Reay Tannahill)

Remember that your characters will talk differently to different people. Their way of talking to a child, for instance, will not be the same as how they talk to adults, and they might abuse or tease close friends or relatives in a way they wouldn't their boss or a stranger.

Checklist

Dialogue has many functions. It should:

◆ provide information
◆ reveal the characters of both speaker and hearer
◆ move the plot forward
◆ show the mood of the speaker
◆ reveal likes and dislikes, attitudes and beliefs
◆ reveal what has happened, and what might happen
◆ create suspense, bring about crises, or solve difficulties.

◆ 'Every line of dialogue should work at least twice.' (Joan Hessayon)

Managing dialogue

You can read it aloud or into a tape recorder to judge whether it sounds real, neither stilted nor too formal.

♦ 'Speak it aloud in front of a mirror (like Dickens).' (Andrew Puckett)

Remember we choose different words and tend to use shorter sentences when we talk, compared with writing.

Your characters will have special habits, ways of speaking, which will help to make them distinctive.

Normally speeches will be short, one thought at a time.

Speakers are identified by tags: 'he said', 'Mary said', 'the doctor said'. The word said is almost invisible, but contrived synonyms such as uttered or related become intrusive. Use alternative words only when they are informative, such as muttered or shouted, though even here the manner of speaking should be obvious from the general atmosphere or the actual words said.

Sometimes it is clear from the order or the context who is speaking, but the occasional reminder keeps the reader on track, and is essential with more than two speakers.

Action points

♦ Write out a conversation with three speakers, making each speaker identifiable without speech tags, by their styles of speech or their opinions.

◆ Listen carefully to people, and note the differences in the way they speak. Look out especially for real, not fictional, foreign and regional speakers on TV or radio, and note the way they may change the orders of words, use different sentence constructions, or use a word which isn't quite right for the meaning.

DISCUSSION POINTS

1. Some bad writing gets published, but that doesn't eliminate the need to make yours as good as possible. Find examples you don't like of overwriting, too much dialect and outdated slang, and try to think of ways of improving them.

2. Analyse short conversations in books and note what every speech does, whether it serves two or more functions.

3. How much formal grammar can you remember from school? Are you aware of any personal quirks or faults? If so make a list. Have you ever consulted a grammar book, or one on style? Do you think doing so might be of help?

6

Setting the Scene

PAYING ATTENTION TO DETAIL

This relates to research, and also to the accuracy and notekeeping which is necessary.

This is where the Internet can prove wonderfully helpful. There is so much information available at any hour of the day or night, without taking trips to libraries, and instead of making copious and laborious notes you can print off useful pages. But there are two things of which to beware:

- Don't assume it is accurate because it is on a website. Not all is. Use the normal research check of consulting more than one authority, and if they differ, consult yet more.

- You can get swamped with paper!

Checklist: places

- Try to visit any real places you use for background.

- Get large-scale maps, check one-way streets and pedestrian precincts, the location of public buildings and hotels. If your story is set in the past get a map as close as possible to the year of the story. There are many sources of maps on the Internet.

- If your characters look out of a window at a distant range of hills, make sure it's possible to see them.

- Check they can catch trains to wherever they're going. Again the Internet has details and timetables.

- Check the time it takes to travel by car or train or bus. If you guess wrongly, someone will know.

If you make a mistake you immediately lose your reader, who will not trust anything else you tell her. Unfortunately quite a few published books do contain mistakes, but that is no excuse for you to have sloppy research. It is obvious you need to check countries and times you are not familiar with, but people make surprising errors about things they *think* they remember, therefore don't bother to check.

Checklist: clothes

- Use clothes, cars and accessories which add to what we know about the characters. They must be realistic.

- If your heroine wears a designer dress is it because:
  (a) she's rich and fashionable
  (b) she bought it in a charity or nearly-new shop, or
  (c) someone, maybe an employer, gave it to her?

- If someone always wears red, or black, or pale pink or scruffy jeans, why? What does it tell us about them? Describing your characters' clothes helps readers to visualise them and know them better, but be careful. Too much detail may be irrelevant and hold up the story.

CHECKING THE FACTS

As well as making sure all the factual detail is accurate, keep notes on details you have invented. This can include background facts which belong to the character profiles, but which you may not have thought of to begin with, such as additional family members, a childhood illness or accident, what they do as the story progresses, what information they have about others, or their beliefs and attitudes. In films continuity staff do this. Make notes as you go, or when re-reading your work.

Checklist: continuity

- Record such permanent details as colours of eyes and hair, and other physical features in your character profiles, so that you can remind yourself when necessary.

- When information is revealed make a note, and also put down which characters already know the facts, or when they learn them, so that you don't have someone acting on the basis of something they couldn't have known.

- Keep track of the time of day, the days of the week, the passing seasons. Make sure the right flowers are blooming, and children are in school in October.

- In some books it feels as though there are a hundred hours in a single day. If you have characters doing a lot make sure it's physically possible for them to fit it into the time. This sounds obvious, but in the excitement of the writing it's easy to overlook.

- Don't let a pregnancy continue for two years.

- If there is a long time-scale keep track of the ages and make sure all the characters age by the same amount.

TEASING THE SENSES

As with other details, use references to what we experience through our senses, to enhance our knowledge of the characters or create a special mood or atmosphere.

The senses most involved will be seeing and hearing, but don't limit yourself to the obvious. Sudden sights of particular things bring back memories, as can hearing a tune or smelling something associated with a previous experience. Use this device to introduce a fact or recollection.

Make the characters active, experiencing things. Show someone stroking velvet, or a cat or a rose petal, or choking on dust, or shivering in the snow, rather than just describing the presence of velvet, or dust or snow.

When using imagery, make it relevant, perhaps echoing the moods of characters, or the style of the book. It can be effective to have a running theme throughout. Some of the more common ones are of the weather, or references to water.

Action point

Whenever you describe something try to see if it could be done more effectively through something a character does.

USING DESCRIPTION AND FLASHBACKS

These are essential devices but they pall with too much use.

Making description unobtrusive

Narrative combines dialogue and description, and the

pace is usually faster during dialogue. Readers may skip long pages of unbroken description, but if it is slipped in as part of the action it is absorbed almost without being noticed, and enhances the scene.

If you want to describe scenery or buildings do it through the eyes of a character who sees it for the first time, or with some powerful emotion such as relief at returning home. The character who notices that a tree has been cut down and opened up some vista, or wanders round a room touching new or familiar objects, can convey so much more, and succinctly, about himself as well as the surroundings, than an outsider's account which can read like an inventory. Much the same applies to seeing people.

Accounts of events are much more dramatic if your characters are directly involved, experiencing them. Your story will be most effective if you mix the straightforward description with dialogue and the reactions of characters.

Hints and suggestions

Often these are more effective than a simple account. The reader can use her own imagination to fill the gaps, and is more involved in the story. She may also have a more vivid imagination than can be provided by any verbal description.

This applies especially to scenes of violence and sex. It can be more horrific to focus on surrounding details of normality than to describe the physical specifics of an execution. It can be more erotic to suggest sexual tension and fulfilment than to go into minute clinical detail, which inevitably becomes repetitive.

♦ 'It's not necessary to include graphic details of violence if you don't feel happy writing them. It's sometimes more effective to suggest, or give just one grisly detail.' (Ann Hulme)

♦ 'Everyone agreed that they dislike the "purple passages" often found in today's novels. Bring back the asterisk!' (Louth Writers' Circle)

Showing, not telling

This is advice frequently given to aspiring writers. Quite simply **showing** means getting inside your characters, and presenting the action and emotion as they experience it. This involves devising scenes. **Telling** is narrating from outside, as if you are the audience looking down on a stage, experiencing everything at second, not first hand. There are times, however, when a little discreet telling is necessary, briefer and better than an awkward, contrived scene which lasts for half-a-dozen swift exchanges.

Exposition

This is a type of description when an explanation is necessary. The writer breaks away from the scene to give the background, some essential information, or a summary of events leading up to it.

It slows the action, and is distancing. Readers will be interested only if they feel it is relevant, and want to know. As with other description it can be more effective if built into the action, but sometimes it would be false if characters amicably discuss something they know perfectly well, like who inherited Aunt Dottie's money. If they are the right sort of people, and it fits your story, you could convey this information by having them row about it. Or they could explain it to a stranger, but only if he has some interest. If these devices are not possible it may have to be simple telling.

Flashbacks

These are scenes from the past, and are often used from a desire to show and not tell. They tend to be overused. They stop the action, can be confusing, and prevent the reader from getting on with the story to come, which is usually more interesting to her.

* 'Not too many flashbacks which interrupt continuity.' (Ruislip Literary Society)

When they are used make certain the reader knows it's a flashback, and when it starts and finishes. A frequent method is to have a character remember something, prompted by what happens now, drop into the flashback scene as if experiencing it, then return to the original scene.

The switch can be within the character's thoughts, as he recalls it, but shown in 'real time' as though it's happening now. Or the character could say something like 'That reminds me of the time when...', and then the flashback drops into real time instead of having the characters talking about it having happened in the past.

It will finish either at the end of a scene or chapter, or if it's a short one contained within another scene, by making it perfectly clear we are back in the main story.

There are various ways of doing this: by referring to the flashback as something in the past, or switching back to a character present in the main scene but not in the flashback, or by picking up the action or conversation which was interrupted by the flashback.

Flashbacks must be interesting in themselves. The reader wants to get on with what's happening *now*, and will lose interest and patience if she is bored by a lengthy flashback which she doesn't perceive as relevant to now.

Action point

Analyse flashbacks in a book, see how each is introduced, how long it is, how it is concluded. Was it necessary or could it have been done differently?

Flashes forward

These are often prologues which are extracts from later in the book, but also can come as hints of future events. They need to be done very carefully as pointers. Have, for example, a character planning what to do or looking forward to better times. Avoid at all costs the heavy-handed authorial interjection of such predictions as 'she didn't know that next year she would have lost everything.'

◆ A pet hate: 'Little did I know that . . .' (Michael Legat)

Foreshadowing

Prepare the ground for future events. Don't throw in new characters, new developments, or solutions to problems, without adequate hints beforehand. As with 'twist in the tale' stories, the ending must be possible, hinted at subtly throughout.

As the story unfolds you may well introduce new characters or situations or subplots. You may need to go back and insert scenes or references to lead into these, or make the eventual appearance less abrupt, more natural.

THE MIDDLE MUST BE COMPULSIVE READING

It can be comparatively simple to write beginnings and ends. Middles distinguish good writers from average ones. You must keep up the momentum of the story, make the reader stay with you, eager to know the outcome. It's fatally easy to lose one's way, having too little to say or padding with more and more incidents which don't help the story.

When I asked what made a good novel, most people said a convincing plot and good characters, but also:

◆ 'One which instructs, reveals, stimulates thought, but above all, entertains. One which leaves a glow. One which you are prepared to recommend to others.' (Andrew Puckett)

◆ 'A fascinating story about likeable, interesting people with whom the reader wants to spend time.' (Margaret James)

◆ 'The narrative needs to flow smoothly so that I am not aware of reading.' (Christine Evans)

◆ 'Intelligently written and plotted.' (Sarah Molloy)

◆ 'Gripping storyline.' (Lynn Sanders)

◆ 'Gripping first chapter.' (Tracy Long)

- 'The plot. This gets me interested but the writing and characters have to be believable or my interest will not be held.' (Mary Wilson)

- 'Setting – either local or exotic settings always popular. Action needs to be plausible as well as exciting – suspension of disbelief.' (Christine Budworth)

- 'Story should keep going at a good pace, not get bogged down by too much description.' (Anne Ambler)

- 'Strong storyline with a fast pace to keep the reader interested.' (Sue Richardson)

- 'When you can't put the novel down.' (Carol Gough)

- 'Keeps the reader turning the pages.' (Deborah Smith)

- 'One that keeps me reading even when there are many more pressing things to do.' (Haydn Middleton)

- 'One which you cannot put down.' (Susan Sallis)

- 'One I want to continue reading.' (Jane Morpeth)

- 'A continuing interest.' (Susan Jones)

- 'Writing that blisters your spirit with delight (a plot that keeps you on tenterhooks until the end).' (Sara Banerji)

- 'One that makes me escape into the world of that novel and makes me believe in the novel itself. I want to continue with that novel.' (Luigi Bonomi)

- 'One that keeps me turning each page to the end.' (Dorothy Lumley)

- 'I like to think it educates me in a subject that interests me.' (Judy Phillips)

- 'One which, after you have finished reading stays in the mind and memory.' (Frederick Nolan)

- 'It has to keep you glued to it either with suspense or in tears.' (Diane Allen)

- 'Something that makes me miss my tube stop.' (Barbara Boote)

- 'A good novel is one that works *for the reader* on every level – and that is nearly always the result of dedicated and detailed technical proficiency; precise control of words, structure and pace, characterisation based on knowledge of what makes people tick, a quality of imaginative vitality that transcends clichés of speech and thought...All these are definable. What isn't definable is the rare and special authorial spark that makes the difference between a competent novel and a brilliant one.' (Reay Tannahill)

Whether you plan the whole story in detail or let your characters and plot develop, you need to be aware of the overall shape. I look at this in the next chapter.

USEFUL REFERENCE BOOKS

As you write more you will build a library of the books used most frequently. Some are general, but you will have special interests depending on the type of novel you write, such as historical or crime. CDs and DVDs are available. On the Internet, you can create an index of 'bookmarks' which will help you to access favourite or frequently used sites quickly. Most writers now use the Internet, but books are still be preferred by many people.

Checklist: books to look for

- A good encyclopaedia and a dictionary, as big as you can afford, are investments. You will be consulting them far more frequently than you imagine.

- One of the yearbooks for writers, the *Writers' and Artists' Yearbook* or *The Writer's Handbook*, even an out of date one, will be of value as both give lengthy lists of agents and publishers.

- Spelling dictionaries are quicker to use than an ordinary one.

- A thesaurus or book of synonyms will help you to avoid repeating words.

- A dictionary of names will give you ideas, and telephone directories are useful in saving you from calling all your minor characters John and Mary Jones.

- A book of quotations can provide ideas and titles.

- Books on grammar, punctuation and style.

- Books by writers about their own experiences and discoveries are useful and often fascinating.

- There are many specialist guides and 'how to' books to help with particular types of writing.

- Maps, guidebooks, and pamphlets, as well as hotel directories, will provide many local details.

- There are numerous small books on a huge variety of subjects, like the Shire books, detailed enough to tell you the basics without being too technical and overwhelming.

- Don't ignore books for children, either. They can be excellent in giving the real core of a subject.

Action point

Look in a large bookshop and make a list of the reference books you would like to acquire. Could these go on a birthday present list?

DISCUSSION POINTS

1. Have you ever spotted a factual or continuity mistake in a book, or wondered whether something could be the way it was described? If so, how would you avoid the mistake?

2. Consider ways in which you can 'show, not tell' your scenes. Will it always work, and if you have to 'tell' can you do it briefly?

3. Do some books sag in the middle? Can you identify the reasons, and say how you would have avoided or got round the problems, to make the books tauter?

The Overall View

AVOIDING WRITER'S BLOCK

There are several versions of this phenomenon, being unable to write, and the solutions depend on the cause.

A traumatic event

An event like a bereavement can be a cause. Know that as time passes you will recover. For some people writing can in itself be healing or a therapy.

Inauspicious surroundings

This is difficult, but P. G. Wodehouse wrote half a novel with his typewriter perched on a suitcase, in the recreation room of a German internment camp surrounded by fifty men singing and playing games, with armed guards peering over his shoulder. He later wrote a chapter while in a police cell in Paris, and a hundred pages in hospital. You too can overcome disadvantages.

Just not feeling in the mood

This could be laziness, a disinclination to work, or have a deeper cause such as not wanting to work on the current project. Overcoming it is up to you and how determined you are to become a writer. Sit down and type (or write) anything. Reply to some letters which have been waiting around. If you have none just type nonsense, shopping lists, or copy some pages from a favourite book, or the last few pages you wrote. The act of typing often stimulates ideas and renewed enthusiasm.

Not knowing how to continue

This may be from lack of ideas, not knowing your characters well enough, too little plot, not enough or not a big enough conflict, or because you have dug yourself into a hole. Reading over what you've done may produce ideas for the next scene. You may need to go back and make changes which will provide the answer. Relax, think about the problem just before you go to bed and let the subconscious work on it. You may have to abandon the project, at least for the moment. If you do, make sure you start something else right away. This will restore your confidence and keep you in practice.

Novelists give suggestions

- ◆ 'Keep going.' (Susan Sallis)

- ◆ 'Keep writing whatever and all problems will pass.' (Sara Banerji)

- ◆ 'Have a stiff gin.' (Anita Burgh)

- ◆ 'A novel's like a car engine. If it stops, then don't swear and bang your fists. Take it apart till you find the fault. If it's repairable, repair it. If it's beyond economical repair, burn it.' (Matthew Kneale)

- ◆ 'If a book blocks, start writing another of a different kind. When lying in bed before sleep, think clearly through a problem. It may solve itself while you sleep.' (Anne Melville)

◆ 'I don't believe in writer's block. There are times when it's harder than others: tough. Who said it was easy to start with? But there is a trick to getting a story moving if it's stuck, and that's to bring in an *important* new character.' (Philip Pullman)

Action point

Make a list of the reasons you've given yourself (or others) for not writing. Were they a hundred per cent truthful? *Creativity isn't the only activity.*

If the muse has deserted you, you can:

1. do research
2. read your notes
3. make more notes
4. tidy your notes or reorganise your filing system
5. go through your file of new ideas
6. make plans for future novels
7. catch up on a host of other 'office' tasks which you don't have time for when being creative.

There is always some work to do, even if it's not writing. Many professionals say writer's block doesn't exist, and journalists with deadlines rarely suffer from it.

DIRECTING YOUR SCENES

Introduce main characters as soon as possible, preferably on the first page, because they are the ones readers want to know about. It's distracting and disappointing to have to switch attention to a different heroine when you assumed the first girl mentioned was the main protagonist.

Bring in all your important characters as soon as the plot allows, as early as you can in the context of the story. Be careful, though, not to introduce too many at once, or the reader becomes confused.

Never introduce any character with a potted biography. Most of their past lives will be irrelevant, and bore the reader. If some of their history is important you can bring in essential facts more subtly, as they are necessary for understanding the character or the situation. Just give a few relevant details which will help the reader remember them, and know why they are there, what their function is.

Don't drop hints or start trails and not follow them. If a one-eyed man looks over the garden wall and recognises the murderer, he must play some future part in the story. Your reader will be waiting for him to return.

Action point
Analyse a book and note when characters are introduced, and how much is said about them

1. then
2. later.

CONTROLLING THE PACE
Pace and rhythm vary from book to book, and within one book. Scenes, action and dialogue are more immediate than description. They create more tension. So does an intensive conflict. Jeopardy is something dire which is being anticipated, but it must be a possible outcome, within the conventions of the genre, to make the reader concerned.

Lots of short sentences and urgent action increase the pace. You can enhance a mood of peace or tension by externals like the weather, a storm or spectacular sunset.

Decide which are the big scenes and work towards them, build up anticipation, and spread them through the book. These scenes should be significant, and change the story or the character. They are likely to be long, so you could have a short, fast scene immediately before for contrast.

Don't stop in the middle of an exciting scene to explain something. You have to get the information in earlier so that the reader understands what's happening and the significance, or explain it later, if you can do so without it appearing like something you forgot to put in.

You can start in the middle of a scene, perhaps a quarrel, to increase the pace.

CONSIDERING THE OVERALL PATTERN

Plots and subplots
There will be one main thread concerning your chief characters, but there could be several subplots. The trick is to weave them all together so that the different strands converge and separate, meet and overlap, affect one another, mirror or contrast one another. Imagine each character as a different coloured ribbon. Some start at the top all tied together, then the ribbons are twisted or plaited together in an irregular way, others being inserted or cut off at different points. They form ever-changing patterns, taking greater or lesser prominence at different times, but

SUMMARY OF CHAPTERS – COBWEB CAGE   (by Marina Oliver)

DATE	Main Chars		
		CHAPTER ONE	P 1
2/1901	M	Marigold alone, Poppy born, locked in pantry	
2/01	MJyMyJ	Johnny finds her – discuss names	
1/05	My	Ivy born – nightmares – flowers – names appropriate	
12/08	J	pit accident	
2/09	My	John home and ill – Mary goes to work	
3/09	P	Poppy wants to go on choir outing	
4/09	M I	Mrs Tasker brings Ivy home with pie – falls on fire.	
		CHAPTER TWO	P 35
4/09	Fam	Ivy's accident – burnt.	
/10	M I	Ivy resists school – effects of burns on John – Johnny delicacies	
3/11	Fam	Ivy draws – job for Marigold – Johnny meat, wants drawing Mary backache	
5/11	Fam	Walk on hills – talk of unions and reforms	
6/11	My	Mary home – pregnant – ill – Mrs Nugent calls – Mary miscarries	
6/11	Jy	Johnny a thief – sent to job in Birmingham.	
		CHAPTER THREE	P 65
3/12	Fam,	Mine strike – army at Cannock	
6/12	Fam	Poppy writes Johnny – Ivy drawing on it – Marigold job at Oxford	
7/12	M	Marigold at Oxford	
10/12	P	Ivy playing with Lizzie – brother says Poppy pretty	
11/12	P	Poppy fantasising about house – wants to get away	
12/12	M R	Marigold helps at dinner party – meets Richard.	
		CHAPTER FOUR	P 95
12/12	Fam	Boxing day – Johnny home – Mary worries losing him, & Poppy	
12/12	M R	Walk with children – meet and talks to Richard	
12/12	R S	Sophia at Baden Baden – Richard recalls why he's at Oxford now	
12/12	I	Ivy playing doctors, breaks window	
12/12	M R	Marigold and Richard walk by river	
12/12	Jy	Johnny at work – tells Lucy about his thieving	
12/12	M R	New Year, Richard drives Marigold home	
		CHAPTER FIVE	P 129
12/12	Fam	Row over window, Ivy denies. Marigold sees poverty at home	
12/12	R	Richard recalls his affair with Flo	
1/13	Fam	John angry – has these attacks, then silent and morose	
1/13	M R	Set off back to Oxford	
1/13	My	Mary sees Marigold in motor car	
2/13	M R	Talk on way back to Oxford – agree to meet again	
2/13	R	Flo demands money because she is pregnant.	

Fig. 6. Keeping track of scenes.

the loose strands are tied, the problems solved or the resolutions found by the end of the book.

Let your readers become familiar with a minor character and interested in him, before you leave the main plot-line to follow his separate story.

Some subplots may be ended quite early, but make sure you don't introduce a subplot, concentrate exclusively on it, and solve it in a few pages. That destroys tension and anticipation. Instead prolong these by inserting bits of the subplot into the main narrative at intervals.

Don't introduce a subplot and forget to continue with it for so long that your readers have forgotten the details by the time you do. If the story demands that it is drawn out, be sure to mention it occasionally.

It helps to keep a list of your scenes, just a few brief words to remind you of what they did and who is taking part. Then you can see quickly if you've left one character or subplot out for too long, or concentrated too much on one subplot for a while at the expense of others.

Viewpoint patterns

When you have a complex plot you will often have a multi-viewpoint pattern, and you need to make smooth transitions from one viewpoint to another. When switching viewpoints make it clear at once, as with flashbacks, that there's a switch. It's very irritating to the reader if the 'he' of the second scene appears to be the same one from the first for several paragraphs.

There are many devices you can use
You can show a transition by a change of time. This can be a straight 'The next day' or a switch from dusk to midday sun.

A change of place can be shown similarly, with a change from a scene in a building to 'Back on the farm' or 'The boat swung broadside as they cast off'.

You can have a lead-in paragraph, such as a speech by a character who wasn't in the earlier scene.

You could have an echo from the first to the next scene, like a repeated word or phrase or action, perhaps by a different character, or you can use simple summary or exposition.

Being consistent
Indicate to the reader early on the pattern of viewpoint switching. If you change with each chapter or scene, do so at once, not halfway through the book, to get the reader accustomed to it.

Tell only what the viewpoint character can see, hear or experience. They can see another character laugh or frown or cry or shout, and assume from this his emotion, but they can't see inside his head and know precisely what he is thinking or what actions he is planning.

Shape
The **shape** of the novel will be a series of crises, each one built up to, then resolved. Some will be small, some huge. The resolution will often lead to a further complication and

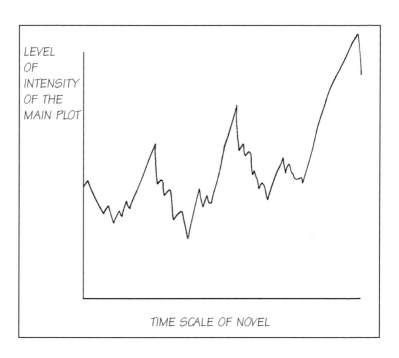

Fig. 7. The peaks and troughs of one plot.

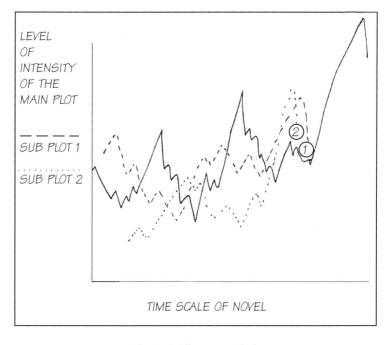

Fig. 8. Adding two subplots.

eventually another crisis, and all will lead to the major crisis or turning point, as close to the end as possible.

For example, there is a problem in the office, an order mislaid, so the boss stays on to sort it. He misses an appointment, or meets an old friend on the later train home. This could have vital consequences such as losing a contract, a row with his wife, the last straw which causes her to walk out, or getting involved in some new development like industrial espionage or witnessing a crime.

You can imagine the plot as a line on a graph, with the level of intensity on one axis, the progress of the novel along the other, and the plot moving in a series of peaks and troughs. If you have one or more subplots they will have similar peaks and troughs, but make sure you don't have all the peaks coming together – spread them out. (See Figures 7 and 8.)

KEEPING THE PAGES TURNING

As the earlier quotes show, authors, agents, editors and readers all say that wanting to get to the end, to see what happens to the characters is essential. They want to be drawn from page to page. It's the sign of a good storyteller when this happens, but storytelling is a difficult skill to learn. There are some pointers, apart from an intriguing plot and good characterisation.

Checklist
Readers will continue if:

- Your characters are interesting.
- What they are doing matters.
- Their aims are laudable.
- You are intriguing the reader, tempting her to want to know more about them and care what happens to them.
- Your plot is exciting, but plausible.
- Your plot has unexpected twists and turns.

Prolonging the suspense

You entice the reader further by continually posing fresh questions, to which she wants the answers, but in giving the answers you pose a further question. Don't explain everything at once. If a girl sees her lover in a compromising situation and he explains how innocent it all was in the next scene, and she believes him, there would be little tension. If the police catch the murderer leaving the scene of the crime covered in blood and carrying the blunt instrument, there is no mystery. If the starship obliterates the competitor in chapter one there is no race.

Suspense is created in this way, also by making promises to your reader, by how the story starts and what expectations you arouse, that the book will be exciting or thrilling. Readers become involved as the characters they like face dangers or suffering. They can be angry at some injustice. The pressure of a time-factor enhances suspense.

Readers keep turning the pages if:

- 'The author is able to generate a sense of excitement and discovery in me.' (Barbara Levy)

- ◆ 'To find the answer to "What happened next".' (Jill Black)

- ◆ There is 'some "mystery": will she get her man, will he escape the hidden menace, will they find the murderer?' (Laura Longrigg)

- ◆ 'Characters, storytelling, humour, writing style.' (Caroline Sheldon)

- ◆ 'Readability. Getting me involved with the characters, caring about them.' (Dorothy Lumley)

- ◆ 'Strong, well written characters with plausible plot.' (Diane Allen)

- ◆ 'Witty, fast writing, a sense of tension and being hooked into various characters.' (Luigi Bonomi)

- ◆ 'Strong characters, and a plot that twists and turns unexpectedly, but never unreasonably.' (Michael Legat)

CLIFFHANGING TECHNIQUES

A favourite way of ending a chapter is the **cliffhanger**, where your characters are left in a desperate situation and the reader, almost without noticing, passes on to the next chapter in order to see what happens. It creates suspense.

You can use the same technique at the ends of scenes. It won't always be explained immediately in the following chapter or scene, which may switch to someone else, but the readers want to go on to find the answer.

You can do it in the middle of a scene by having interrupted events or conversations, unexplained hints and references, surprises, alternative possibilities with the choices not made at once.

WRITING A SATISFYING ENDING

Agents, editors and readers want to be able to put a book down with a sigh of satisfaction.

◆ 'When I finish that novel I feel a sense of completeness and deep satisfaction.' (Luigi Bonomi).

In some literary novels the outcome is hinted at rather than explained, and can be downbeat. In most other novels endings tend to be upbeat, and it's more satisfying for the reader to know what happened. Did the hero get the girl, the detective unmask the crook, the explorer return safely, the soldiers win the battle? How were these resolutions finally concluded?

Make certain all the ends you want to tie up are satisfactorily explained, and you haven't overlooked some vital piece of evidence in your relief at finishing.

A satisfying ending is not necessarily a happy one, but it must be logical, follow from what has gone before. You can connect the ending to the beginning with some allusion or repetition, but most endings reach a climax, the protagonists achieve some ambition, get what the reader feels they deserve after all their trials and endeavours.

Before you give your protagonists their ending, clear up all the other strands, tuck them in, and get the other characters off-stage. Leave the stage clear for this final scene, and make it a scene, action rather than discussion. Include essential explanation within the scene.

DISCUSSION POINTS

1. Take your plot, or one you know well, and draw a diagram similar to the ones in this chapter of the peaks and troughs of the main plot and any subplots.

2. Look at how you can insert essential information. Does dialogue, narrative, or straight exposition work best, or does it depend on the novel?

3. Analyse the endings of ten books you have read recently, and say why they are (or are not) satisfying.

8

Submitting Your Work

FINAL POLISHING

You've reached the end of your novel. Well done. You thought you had almost finished? I'm sorry, but there is still a great deal to do.

Don't spend too much time as you go

It's a great temptation to keep going back over what you've done. You can always find things to change. Even when a script has been completed, writers tinker. They are perhaps reluctant to let it go out into a hard, hostile world.

Try not to go back too much while doing the first draft, unless you get to a complete dead end and have to alter something vital for the plot to work. It's better to finish your first draft, prove you can write a whole novel, then start revising. Some writers revise as they go, but many do a very fast first draft and spend far longer on the revising stage. The experienced writer knows that revision, whenever done, is the most important, often most difficult task. Most writers I spoke to did three or more drafts.

- 'Write huge and cut harshly.' (Sara Banerji)

Taking a break

Put the script away for as long as possible, then come

back refreshed. You can have a blitz on garden or housework, or go out and see all the friends you've been neglecting.

Keep on writing though. It's fatally easy to get out of the habit. You can write something else, short stories or non-fiction. Distance yourself from your novel, try to forget it, so that when you come back you can judge it objectively. Then try to read it as if you are new to the story.

Now for the really hard work
Revision can be done at several levels, and it's very like the editing and copy-editing before a book is published.

You can start with the details, which is what a copy-editor does, or the overall view, the editor's task.

Action points: correcting details
It's perhaps easiest at first to concentrate on:

1. Simple corrections of typing errors.

2. The changing of words which have been repeated too close together, or too often.

3. The removal of superfluous adverbs and adjectives, often replacing these phrases with more appropriate or effective verbs and nouns.

4. Checking for clichés, trite expressions, or convoluted metaphors.

As you are doing this you may want to:

5. Change the order of words or passages.

6. Rewrite sentences.

7. Shift scenes around.

Checklist

Make sure everything is essential and important.

- Now might be the best time for a swift read-through, making notes as you go.

- Have you started in the right place, or too soon in the story?

- Look at each scene for its purpose. Does it move the story forward, demonstrate facets of character, tell the reader something relevant and new? If not, why is it there?

- Does the action come in the wrong place? Is the dialogue natural, interesting, necessary, informative? If not you may have to cut it out.

- You can do the same for each sentence. Cut out everything that isn't essential.

- Does the pace vary enough?

- Are some scenes too slow or boring?

- Have you exploited every situation and emotion fully?

- Is there too much exposition?

- Is anything missing, such as explanations or clues?

- Have you always chosen the right viewpoint or would a scene be better done from a different one?

- Are there too many flashbacks?

- Have you made it clear when you change viewpoint and have flashbacks?

- Are your big scenes in the right places?

- Does the story flow, the events easily understood by the reader?

- Is the resolution satisfactory, arising inevitably out of the story?

- Is every character essential? Could two minor ones be merged?

- Are the characters real, convincing?

- Are they in conflict?

- Do they develop, grow?

- Is their behaviour in line with their motivations?

- Check all the details, make sure you have been consistent, that the time-scale is correct.

- Is the language appropriate? Is it vivid and arresting?

- Have you used the senses?

- Is there any humour?

- Have you used active verbs?

- Have you used specific rather than general examples?

When you are satisfied with every aspect and have a clean, corrected copy using the accepted layout as described earlier, you are ready to submit your work.

USING AN AGENT

Many authors do very well without an agent, but it is much easier to have one. Many publishers will not even consider unsolicited scripts, sending them straight back. Always check before sending your script to a publisher yourself that they will consider it. The problem is that it can be as difficult to find an agent as it is to get the script accepted by a publisher. Both agents and publishers are in business, and need to pay their way. They must become good judges of what will sell if they want to remain in business.

Agents are in regular touch with editors and know what they like, or are looking for. Editors, knowing that agents will only pass on what they think is publishable, take submissions from agents more seriously than unsolicited ones. Agents negotiate contracts, and can sort out any later problems. They charge a percentage of your earnings, but usually get more for you to cover this.

Finding an agent

The ideal way is by recommendation through an existing client, but you won't necessarily know published writers and their agents may not be prepared to take on more clients.

There are lists in the yearbooks, and on the Internet, and they often indicate whether agents specialise in particular types of work, names of some clients, whether they are accepting new clients, and if they want a query letter first.

Agents attend conferences, and give talks and workshops. You can meet them this way, though you won't be popular if, as at least one aspiring writer did, you pursue them into the loo and thrust scripts under the cubicle door. If you can find a new one just setting up, you might be taken on before their list is full.

Action point

Go through one of the yearbooks and make a list of at least ten prospective agents you might try.

ENTERING COMPETITIONS

The yearbooks and writing magazines have details of prizes, some open to unpublished writers. There are often special conditions, such as a minimum or maximum age, or a regional connection. While the number of entries for these competitions can be in the hundreds, winning one is valuable for publicity as well as any monetary reward. Sometimes runners-up as well as winners are offered publishing contracts.

There are many Internet sites which have news of competitions, or even run them. But be cautious before you send money as an entrance fee. Make sure it is a genuine competition. Promises of publication on the Net sound good, but unless it is a prestigious organisation which runs the site, this is unlikely to bring in either money or publicity.

Action point

Make lists of competitions you would be eligible for.

CHOOSING THE RIGHT PUBLISHER

When writing a novel you can write what you like and think about publication later, or aim your work at a particular publishing house from the start. Which you choose depends on the type of novel.

If you aim to write category fiction, romance novels for Harlequin Mills and Boon, for instance, you have to abide by very strict guidelines as to length, limits on the number of main characters, concentration on relationships and so on. The publishers send out guidelines for potential authors but send a stamped A4 self-addressed envelope if you want any of these. There are many such publishers of category romances in the USA, and they all want different things, so you need to know their requirements first or your chances of success are minimal.

◆ 'Be professional: do your homework – submit work to a house which publishes material of the same nature as your own.' (Deborah Smith)

◆ Do your 'market research, then use your own voice.' (Elizabeth Johnson)

◆ 'Select the publisher on the basis of the kind of books they publish.' (Richard Todd)

◆ 'My first published novel was rejected by fourteen publishers before being accepted. Conclusion: Determination is just as important as talent. (It would have helped, of course, to have taken more care in the choice of a suitable publisher.)' (Anne Melville)

Many publishers have several imprints, each usually publishing a limited range or type of book.

Action point
Make a list of the most likely publishers for your novel.

As with agents, there are sometimes new publishers and new imprints which will not have a ready-made list of authors, and will be more willing to consider newcomers. To hear about these opportunities you need to mix with other writers, to read the specialist magazines, to network. Where better to do this now than the Internet? There are hundreds of groups of writers online, and we will look at the options in the next chapter.

PREPARING PROPOSALS, OUTLINES AND SYNOPSES
Query letters
If an agent or publisher specifies a preliminary letter, send it. Post, don't fax it. Some agents will answer initital queries by email. Anything else may come back unread and you will have wasted your postage. Always send return postage and a self-addressed envelope or label.

The letter is your introduction, the first impression the agent or editor will have of you, so it is important to make it as good as possible.

◆ 'The cover letter is more important (than the title).' (Barbara Levy)

◆ I am looking for 'professionalism in submission letter and presentation.' (Barbara Boote)

◆ 'Be professional in your approach to selling.' (Judy Piatkus)

It should be business-like, no more than a page, single spaced, saying what you have written, a two or three sentence summary of it, any relevant facts about yourself such as previous publications or special knowledge, and asking whether you might send sample chapters for consideration. You might add a reason for choosing that firm, to show you've done your homework, on the lines of they represent or publish lots of crime novelists and your script is a crime novel. But never flannel. Gushing, or sycophantic praise, will annoy rather than impress.

◆ I dislike authors 'trying to queue-jump, trying to get my attention by being rude, controversial or fawning in submission letters.' (Jane Morpeth)

Proposals

These are more likely to be required for non-fiction than for novels. Occasionally established authors may be commissioned on a proposal and a few chapters only for a novel, and one day you may need to make one.

Editors and agents have varying policies on accepting manuscripts on the basis of proposals. Agents are, perhaps understandably, more willing to try.

◆ 'If I thought it was good enough.' (Carole Blake)

- Yes 'but they would usually have to complete it before a publisher would be interested.' (Sarah Molloy)

- 'Unlikely.' (Jane Morpeth)

- 'Rarely. If highly commended by an agent, if a celebrity author.' (Barbara Boote)

- 'Probably only if the writer had a track record in another area, say journalism or TV.' (Barbara Levy)

and:

- 'Never. A few good chapters do not make a book. Many writers start off well and fall away, or appear to lose interest midway through a novel.' (Bob Tanner)

Proposals include an **outline**, a **synopsis**, a list of **contents** and **chapter headings**, and details of where you see the book fitting into the existing market.

Outlines

This is a very brief description, one page, of the story. It is something you might do when planning the story, with the chapters indicated and the main scenes listed.

Action point

For an exercise, do a proposal and outline for the book you have finished.

Synopses

These are quite different, and it is essential you study the art of writing them.

- ◆ (I like) 'a very easy to understand synopsis written in a clear style.' (Luigi Bonomi)

A synopsis should accompany your script, especially if you send a **partial**, that is the first few chapters only. A summary should be in narrative form, usually the present tense, two to four A4 pages double-spaced. They can be important to get you past the first hurdle.

Some agents prefer submissions in a different form. Carole Blake, for example, in her book *From Pitch to Publication*, asks for a brief blurb, a separate list of character biographies, and a synopsis of four to ten pages telling the story.

The synopsis is a practical aid to selling your script. It must tell the whole story and the conclusion. It is not, as many inexperienced writers believe, the same as the cover blurb which is designed to intrigue potential readers.

Checklist
A synopsis should include:

1. an explanation of the background
2. the setting in place and time
3. who the main characters are
4. what they are like
5. the theme
6. the main areas of conflict
7. a mention of the major scenes and crises
8. important subplots
9. how the story ends.

That's the simple part.

Checklist

The synopsis should also convey to an editor:

- the mood
- the style of writing
- any special qualities in your writing, such as humour or lyricism
- whether there is enough plot for the length
- whether the plot progresses
- that you can maintain interest after the first few chapters.

Even if some of the other things in your story or first few chapters are not right, a good professional synopsis might persuade an editor to look at the rest of your novel, to see if it has enough to make working on it a practical option. It could make her encourage you to try again, this time with a better idea of what is wanted by that particular publisher, and a known editor to send it to.

MULTIPLE SUBMISSIONS

This means sending the script simultaneously to more than one publisher. It is being done more now, especially in America, and saves time while waiting for responses, but some publishers refuse to consider it, so check first.

You must say you have sent to others, and if one publisher makes an offer which you accept you must immediately tell the others that the script is sold.

It could save time to send several query letters at once, but make them personal, not a circular which will be binned. You can take up the first favourable response, but the same rules of courtesy apply, you let the others know the position. Publishing is a relatively small world, and gaining a bad reputation is easier than losing one.

How long to wait?

Replies can normally be expected within one to three months, but don't be too impatient. Never pester agents or editors. They don't want authors who might prove difficult.

- ◆ 'If this happens, it almost invariably results in an immediate rejection.' (Luigi Bonomi)

Pet hates were:

- ◆ 'Prospective writers who want to meet me before I've had a chance to see something they've written.' (Barbara Levy)

- ◆ 'Authors who want to meet before I've read their work.' (Carole Blake)

Coping with rejections

You will almost certainly get them, and it hurts, but there are many reasons apart from the quality of the writing, and you have to try again and again.

- ◆ The agent or editor simply does not have room for another client or book.

- They may already have writers who produce similar books and want to have a more varied list.

- That particular slot in a publisher's list is already filled, and they don't want more.

- Editors may have accepted a similar book recently, and they won't want too many of a particular type.

- They may have bought more than usual recently, and have a backlog.

- In the end the judgement is subjective, and these days scripts have to appeal to both hardback and paperback editors, as well as the marketing department.

When your script comes back you are entitled to feel miserable, but don't throw it in the wastepaper basket or the back of a cupboard. In a day or so you will be able to assess any comments more calmly. A formal rejection, even if it is a full-page letter, tells you nothing. Any personal comment, however brief, means the editor was interested enough to try and help. Take notice. If more than one person makes the same sort of comment, take even more notice and consider whether you need to make changes.

It's best to get on with some other project meanwhile, and you can send out the script again. At some point you can go back to it and decide whether to make changes. But if you get some encouraging feedback, and believe in it yourself, persevere.

DISCUSSION POINTS

1. Do you remember discussing English literature at school, and looking beneath the surface for hidden meanings, or discussing clever and apt language? If you reread your own work after a while, do you see in it similar things which you hadn't realised were there?

2. Are you prepared to be patient, trying several agents or publishers, without giving up? How will you select appropriate ones?

3. Would you be willing to do yet more revisions and rewriting if an editor asked you to? What value do you think an editor's suggestions would have?

4. Practise writing blurbs and synopses of published books you have enjoyed.

9

Working with Other Writers

DIFFERENT METHODS

You can work with other writers at a distance, by reading books and magazines. Reading advice manuals or receiving a monthly magazine might be a stimulus to your writing, but the disadvantage is that you get no feedback.

There is feedback with correspondence courses, critical assessment of your work and suggestions for improvement.

The real buzz, however, comes from personal contacts with other writers. This can be done through classes, groups, or special conferences. You can join 'communities' on the Internet. These are international and can take different forms:

♦ courses from beginners to post-graduate levels

♦ regular newsletters which you may or may not be able to contribute to

♦ bulletin boards where messages can be posted

♦ chat groups where you can 'chat' online with others

♦ small groups whose members can email one another,

exchange manuscripts and critiques, or discuss problems.

The majority of writers find that just discussing problems, or even moaning to fellow writers who have the same problems, is a tremendous help in proving you are not alone.

The value of these contacts is felt by many writers.

- ◆ 'Encouragement and criticism (is) useful – (I have had) much useful advice.' (Clare Knight)

- ◆ 'Draws attention to mistakes, and I find advice helpful, but it can be nit-picking.' (Diana Atkinson)

- ◆ 'Mutual support – constructive criticism.' (Zoë March)

BOOKS AND MAGAZINES

Writers' and Artists' Yearbook
This is published annually and has lists of book and magazine publishers, with addresses, special imprints, names of editors, sometimes details of what is wanted such as preliminary letter or first three chapters.

As well as lists of agents there are sections for overseas markets, and information on publishing topics.

The Writer's Handbook
This is a similar annual publication with lists, information on specific publishers and agents, and articles. Both have lists of societies and prizes, and some courses.

Action point

Look at both books before you decide which to buy, since the details about agents or publishers may be more relevant to your needs in one rather than the other. Libraries will have copies, and you may find a second-hand one, but check names, addresses and requirements in the latest edition and directly with the firm before sending a manuscript. There are frequent changes of address and personnel and these details can be out of date before the yearbooks are published.

Magazines

The first four magazines listed below are for beginners, containing hints and factual information. The other two are trade publications read by editors, agents, librarians and booksellers. Some extracts are now online.

The New Writer
Published bi-monthly with news, articles, tips, letters, and occasional poetry and fiction.

Writing Magazine
A monthly magazine available through newsagents. It has interviews with writers and others in the publishing world, articles, details of competitions, a help column, letters page, and advertisements of courses and other services to writers.

Writers' News
A monthly subscription magazine, which has market and publishing news. It includes *Writing Magazine*.

Writers' Forum
Similar to the last one, bi-monthly, with short fillers and longer articles on all aspects of writing.

The Bookseller
A weekly magazine for the book publishing trade, well worth consulting in libraries, with details about people, publishing houses and the books they publish.

Publishing News
A weekly newspaper with information on books and publishers.

JOINING HOME STUDY COURSES
The magazines advertise correspondence courses. There are several for novelists.

These courses are ideal if you want to work at your own pace, receiving qualified comments on your work. Choose a course where you pay as you go, not one where you will be expected to send a large sum to begin with.

Thanks to the Internet you can work one-to-one with tutors, at any level. Courses may be organised in various ways, such as working at your own pace, weekly lessons and assignments, or in groups where other members of the group comment on your work, and the tutor comments on these as well as the original. Many universities, especially in America, are offering higher-level courses online.

OBTAINING PROFESSIONAL CRITICISM
It may be more constructive, if you have already written a novel, to have it assessed individually. Some agents who charge a reading fee will give a short comment, but for a detailed **critique** you need to pay a specialist.

People who run these services can be practising writers, tutors, publishers' readers, former agents or editors, perhaps working from home while they have young children, or retired.

Criticism services are offered by writing schools and independent agencies such as the one I run, Storytracks. They advertise in the yearbooks and writing magazines. Many agencies now have websites advertising their services. It is sensible if you can to get a personal recommendation, but if you don't know anyone to ask, check the qualifications of the critic and make sure they know the current publishing world. Also ask how much they charge and what they will give you for this. For example, at Storytracks we are all published authors and you know who will read your typescript.

NETWORKING
This includes gathering knowledge and getting to know people who may impart hot tips about a new agent or publisher long before it's in any magazine. This information can spread within hours over the Internet.

Finding books and magazines is easy, but how do you go about contacting other writers?

JOINING WRITERS' GROUPS
There are national, regional, local and postal groups, as well as online computer circles on the Internet.

National groups
Mainly for published writers. General ones are the Society of Authors, PEN, and The Writer's Guild, with sub-groups for specialists.

There are organisations for particular genres: the Crime Writers Association which admits published writers, the Romantic Novelists' Association which has a scheme for critiquing the scripts of unpublished members, and the British Fantasy Society which is open to readers as well as writers. Details are in the yearbooks.

Many of these groups have their own websites where you can gather information, and some have Internet discussion groups for members. A few local groups have websites, and more will no doubt appear.

Regional groups

Groups such as Southern Writers, or West Country Writers, or the Union of Welsh Writers, are mainly for published writers, but not always. It's worth asking.

Local groups

These vary enormously, from a few people all engaged on the same type of writing to groups with over a hundred members. Most groups meet regularly to read and discuss work, which provides valuable criticism. You need to evaluate the criticism, and know whether it is fair and reliable. The majority of members have published very little, but many published writers and knowledgeable people belong to them, and they are good places to start with. Make sure your aims are the same as theirs. Be wary of unstinting praise: some groups are mutual admiration societies. Others are mainly social.

Groups often have speakers, which is a good way to begin networking. Even if the speaker is not in your own line you can usually pick up hints on methods of work, or research, or simply absorb more information about publishing, all of it adding to your total knowledge.

Libraries will have details of groups in your area.

Postal groups
Postal groups circulate work and add comments before passing it on. If you can't get out to meetings this is the next best way of being in touch with other writers. Some people prefer it, since it allows more time for studying a piece of writing before passing judgement on it.

Online groups
There are many of these which can do anything from simple discussions about books and writing, to mutual critiquing of manuscripts.

Start your own
If there is no suitable group near you consider starting your own. Local radios and newspapers are often willing to give free publicity, and nearby libraries and bookshops might put up notices.

Use Internet message boards
On these you can post queries or opinions and get ideas. There are vast numbers, so try several to find those of interest or use.

Action point
Make a list of possible groups you might join.

♦ 'Published novelists get sacked, lose readers, write books that bomb, lose faith in themselves. But what keeps me going is knowing other authors, knowing that what happens to me also happens to them.' (Margaret James)

◆ Consider whether you can offer to work for a group. This way you get to know writers quickly.

ATTENDING COURSES, WORKSHOPS AND WEEKENDS

You could take a first degree or a PhD in writing. Over half of British higher education institutions run full-time courses as well as evening classes, day or weekend schools.

Local education authorities, regional arts councils, writers' groups and commercial organisations run courses. Most are for comparatively small groups and there will be a mixture of talks, discussions and workshop exercises. A few are huge conventions, with many different activities going on at the same time. Lists are in the yearbooks, or can be supplied by libraries and arts councils.

You can often find workshops held in conjunction with literary festivals. Writers come to talk at these festivals and it's a good opportunity of meeting them.

Conventions

These are like conferences, but the emphasis is more on readers meeting writers than being mainly for writers. The Crime Writers and Waterstones run Dead on Deansgate in the UK. A similar international event is Boucheron, usually held in America. The magazine *Romantic Times* holds an annual convention, usually in America. Science fiction and fantasy writers and fans can meet at various conventions worldwide.

RESOURCES ON THE INTERNET

Many of the above organisations and publications have websites containing more up-to-date information than the printed material, though you need to subscribe to some. Many also have archives with articles of interest to writers, interviews and essays.

Action point

Begin to collect details of courses advertised, and contact addresses, and decide which would suit you best.

DISCUSSION POINTS

1. Read copies of writing magazines and decide if you want to subscribe. Which would be most suitable for you?

2. Read at least two copies of *The Bookseller*, and look for items of use to you, now or in the future.

3. What sort of criticism do you think would be useful to you, and where could you obtain it?

(10)

Being Published

CONTRACTS, COPYRIGHT AND LEGAL MATTERS

Contracts

These cover **monetary details** such as how much is paid and when, **second rights**, **author's free copies**, **remaindering**, and what happens if there is a dispute. Contracts may be a single page or a dozen closely typed pages. It's advisable to consult an expert, and this is one job agents do. The Society of Authors will also advise.

Copyright

Despite recent 'tidying' legislation in the UK the law of **copyright** is extremely complicated. It varies in different countries, and there is a mass of case law which makes trying to interpret the fine details a specialist task. Because of this, infringements of copyright and subsequent court battles can be very expensive.

To give the simplest possible explanation, copyright applies to an author's rights in his work, which exist as soon as he has written it, before publication. This means that other people cannot quote from a piece of work without the author's permission. It applies to lines of songs, or extracts from broadcast scripts. There are exceptions, such as quoting short extracts for purposes of illustration or comment or study, but it would be wise to consult a lawyer before publishing anything you haven't permission to quote. There is no copyright in ideas or titles.

In the UK since January 1996 copyright extends for seventy years after an author's death. A new edition can create a new copyright, so just because an author died over seventy years ago it does not necessarily mean their work is out of copyright and can be quoted freely.

You can give away copyright, and some publishers may ask for this, but it is not a good idea to agree.

Contracts specify which rights an author grants to a publisher, for example first British, paperback, large print, translation, audio, film and so on. With the possibility of publishing books on the Internet, electronic rights have become the subject of many discussions.

Normally rights revert to the author after a period when the book is out of print, but with the advent of machines which can print and bind single copies from computer disks, books can always be 'in print', and this is another area for discussion.

Other legal matters

Libel
If something is defamatory and published in a permanent form, such as in writing, it may constitute **libel**. An action for damages can be brought. If you take a living person as a model for your villain, and give him derogatory sayings or actions, you could be in trouble. It's wise to check there isn't a clergyman or accountant with the same name in the

town where you set your story, or anyone who might, by great similarity of name, be assumed to be him.

Plagiarism
Ideas, plots and themes are bound to be duplicated since there are limited numbers of them, but **plagiarism** consists of a deliberate copying from another person's work and pretending it is your own.

THE PROCESS OF PUBLICATION

It normally takes a year from acceptance of the script to publication, and the author has quite a lot to do still, apart from writing the next novel. There will normally be editorial decisions and consultations, and **proof reading**. The publisher will organise jackets and publicity.

The editor's work

A good editor knows her firm, what it wants, and how to achieve it. Her input is immensely valuable, as she comes to the manuscript with a fresh eye, isn't so deeply enmeshed in the detail as the author is, and can see where changes will improve the whole. A good writer wants to be published and will comply with editorial suggestions, or consider them seriously and perhaps make alternative suggestions to achieve the same objective.

- ◆ 'An average manuscript from a new author does need quite a large amount of editing, often two to three sets of revisions need to be carried out.' (Luigi Bonomi)

- ◆ 'Varies.' (Judy Piatkus)

- ◆ 'Varies dramatically.' (Barbara Boote)

- 'Can vary from no work to many drafts.' (Beverley Cousins)

- 'An author's publisher is, in effect, his/her very first, critical, perhaps over-critical, reader. If something strikes your publisher (who *is* on your side) as not very good, then it may have the same effect on other readers – the buying public, who are not on your side until your book persuades them that they should be.' (Reay Tannahill)

- 'A good editor is worth her weight in gold. Listen to what he/she has to say!' (Joan Hessayon)

The copy-editor's work

After the editor has discussed or suggested changes, the copy-editor will check details. Make sure you see these changes, as occasionally copy-editors will make some you may disagree with, and this needs to be resolved now, since changes after typesetting can be very expensive.

- 'Most authors can do with a hand over spelling, punctuation, ambiguities, infelicities, inconsistencies.' (Michael Legat)

Then the book will be sent for **typesetting**, or increasingly these days, set from a **computer disk**. **Proofs** will usually come as **double-page spreads**, or **bound** in a paper cover, about six to four months before publication date. The author will need to go through these mainly for typing errors. Learn the common proof reading symbols.

BOOK JACKETS

Meanwhile an artist will have been commissioned to design the jacket. You may or may not be asked for suggestions. Some imprints have a common format which is instantly recognisable on the shelves. You may be fortunate to be shown the jacket as it progresses from a drawing to a painting, and asked for comments.

The jackets are used for publicity before the actual books are ready. As well as the cover picture there will be the blurb on the inside front flap which you, the editor, or a special department will be asked to write. This must be designed to tempt the browser into buying or borrowing your book. On a paperback the blurb will be on the outside back cover. Details of the author will usually appear on the back inside flap, and review quotes of this or earlier books somewhere too.

Both librarians and booksellers considered jacket, blurb and title mattered a great deal when they selected books, though readers thought they mattered less.

'I often don't agree with the blurbs' (Anne Donnelly).

This is probably because readers tended to choose books on the basis of their familiar, favourite authors, or the recommendation of friends. For the new writer's books to be in the library or bookshop, available for choice, their titles and blurbs and jackets need to be good.

Action point
Practise writing intriguing blurbs for books you have read.

PUBLICITY IN MANY GUISES
- 'Publicity is more important than a good review.' (Ralph James)
- 'I often don't agreee with the blurbs.' (Anne Donnelly)

Other booksellers from both small independents and large chains agreed that advertising influenced sales, though 'word of mouth' (Richard Carr) and 'recommendations and "Book at Bedtime"' (Brian Pattinson) were important. Television and radio book programmes are increasingly influential.

The final copies will come a month or so before publication, and there is nothing which compares with the thrill of holding your first real book in your hands, unless it's holding your new baby. In many ways a book *is* a baby in that it has taken a long time to produce, and will need constant nurturing for some time yet.

Publishers will have advertised the book, sent out review copies, and tried to get your local papers, magazines and radio stations interested. The launch parties, signings in Harrods, national newspaper reviews, publicity tours and TV chat show appearances happen to very few.

Getting your own publicity

You can do a lot yourself. Some of these suggestions are expensive, but others cost little more than a few postage stamps. What you do must depend on how much you can afford, and whether you feel it is worth your while in terms of present sales, or publicity in the hope of future sales.

On most Internet bookstores you can write about your books, and this will be put on the site where potential readers can see it. You can get your friends to write reviews which will be posted there too.

Your own website

Many Internet service providers allow subscribers free space to display their own material on the Internet. You can pay an expert to design one, or you can create a simple site yourself. There is a special language called hyper text mark up language (HTML) which allows you to put in fonts and formatting. There is also special software to help you do this, and the more recent word processing programs will convert for you. As long as you are connected to the Internet you do not need to be an expert or to pay out lots of cash if all you want is to advertise your books.

Blogs

A simpler method is to construct a web diary, or blog. Go to *www.blog.com* for advice and templates.

Action points: publicity suggestions

1. Send press releases to your local papers, magazines and radio stations, and try to get them to interview you.

2. Visit local bookshops and try to persuade them to stock and display your books. If they get them, they may be happy for you to sign copies.

3. Offer to talk to local groups. Many organisations are always eager to know about speakers, especially if you offer to do it just for expenses and a chance to sell your books at the meeting. Most publishers will be happy for you to buy books at a discount for this purpose.

4. Draft leaflets to send to your friends, leave in libraries, or bookshops, or hand out at meetings. Typed and photocopied onto coloured paper they are effective.

Fig. 9. Publicity aids you can organise.

5. Throw yourself a launch party, and make sure you have copies to sell to your guests.

6. Have self-adhesive labels printed to put on your correspondence.

7. Have postcards or bookmarks printed, more or less elaborate, to give away.

8. If you are on the Internet, write comments for the bookstores.

9. Visit other authors' websites and think about what you want on your own. Begin to design one.

Reviews

Librarians and booksellers all read reviews, and are influenced by them. Fewer readers read them.

♦ 'I am also influenced by book programmes on TV and radio (but) to some extent this depends on the reviewer and indeed the style of the review.' (Mary Brackley)

♦ 'I *am* influenced by reviews, and may borrow/request books from the library accordingly.' (Frances Hawkins)

A minute proportion of published novels is reviewed nationally, so don't expect much publicity from that. You will have more chance of a review in the local press, so cultivate your local journalists.

Regular reviewers do about one book a week, and some have little choice about which books they do. Others have complete freedom to choose. Most told me that they tend to review established authors: 'There are more of them' (F. E. Pardoe), but some will select new writers.

What reviewers liked

◆ 'Subject matter.' (Rebecca Abrams)

◆ 'A well written, good plot.' (Sarah Broadhurst)

◆ 'That it should engage my interest: and fairly quickly!' (F. E. Pardoe)

◆ 'Good quality in the actual writing, as the lack of it can undermine absolutely every other merit the novel might have.' (Anon)

◆ 'The writing style, then character.' (Anon)

They disliked:

◆ 'Reading the same book the author has written before, or borrowed from someone else. Lack of originality.' (F. E. Pardoe)

A reviewer told me that space is so precious that authors should use any contacts they have to get reviews! It's a jungle, but if you can get in, do.

This is depressing for a new writer. A few immensely fortunate ones do get publicity at the start, but for most it's a hard slog. The only way to break in is to produce books regularly, and build up a readership by word of mouth.

ADVANCES, ROYALTIES AND SUBSIDIARY RIGHTS

Advances
Advances are the sums paid before the book is published, or on publication. These will normally be in two parts, one half on signature of contract, one half on publication, but there are variations on this.

Royalties
Royalties are paid once or twice a year, and are normally a percentage of the retail price of the book. Usually the terms are 10 per cent on hardback, less on paperback editions. If sales are high there may be a higher royalty, 12.5 per cent or 15 per cent on sales above a specified quantity. Sometimes with high volume sales at big discounts this may be the percentage of the publisher's receipts, and with 40 per cent or 50 per cent discounts to booksellers this can be far less than authors imagine.

However, the situation has been confused by the breakdown of the **Net Book Agreement**, which means that there is no enforceable selling price.

The advance is set against earnings, so until the book has earned that amount you will receive no more royalties.

Subsidiary rights
Subsidiary rights are the sales for different editions, usually paperback or hardback when to a different publisher, or large print or audio editions. They also cover the sales for translation or to America, to book clubs or for serialisation, condensation or digest, and dramatisation rights for radio, TV or film. There are others, but these are the main ones you are likely to encounter at first.

PUBLIC LENDING RIGHT

This is a payment from a government agency based on the number of times books are borrowed from libraries. There is an upper limit which a small proportion of writers reach every year, but the extra income is welcomed by many writers whose books have been published solely in library editions and are rarely available in bookshops unless by special order. It is the responsibility of the author to register in the first place, and to register every new title or edition as it is published.

ALLOWABLE EXPENSES

Keep accounts

Your income, even after publication, will come in just a few times a year, once or twice for the advance, perhaps twice for royalty payments, once for Public Lending Right, and maybe other payments for second rights.

Your expenditure, however, may be daily. Note postage and telephone calls, stationery costs, books and magazines you buy to do with writing or research, travel costs and meals you buy when away from home. Keep receipts where you have them.

Working out expenses

You can offset allowable expenses against income. Those above, which are directly applicable to your writing, are straightforward, but you may be asked, if you use your computer for other purposes, for example, to make an apportionment of the percentage it is used for writing.

Income		£	Expenditure		£
Jan	Advance, Bk 4	1,000	Jan	Post	3
				Phone	6
				Paper	20
				Subscriptions	10
					30
					8
				2 days away	100
Feb	PLR	650	Feb	Post	10
				Phone	9
				Padded envps	5
				Typing chair	150
Mar	Fee for talk	50	Mar	Post	5
	Large print advance	400		Phone	7
				Books	30
Apr	Royalties, Bks 1&2	845	Apr	Post	8
				Phone	3
				Env. folders	10

Fig. 10. Simple income and expenditure records.

There are other less obvious expenses which may be allowable. If you do research while on holiday, for instance, a proportion of your costs, entry charges into museums, and guide books and maps, could be allowed. You can charge part of the telephone rental charges, and part of your heating and lighting costs. Subscriptions to writing organisations, and travel to their meetings, are allowable as are fees for courses.

INCOME TAX AND VAT

You will be liable for income tax on your 'profit': income minus allowable expenses.

Don't set aside one room for writing, or there could be capital gains tax implications if you sell your house.

You will need to distinguish between running expenses and capital expenditure on equipment and furniture. A proportion of the latter can be set against profits each year. However, the rules can and do change, sometimes every year. Do consult your tax office, which will send you appropriate leaflets.

At first simple accounts and a sympathetic taxman will be all you need, but as your success builds your tax affairs will become more complicated, and it may be worth employing an accountant. Some firms specialise in advising authors, and the Society of Authors can provide names and addresses.

Value Added Tax

This applies to writers with a higher income, as with other businesses, but by the time you reach this level you will almost certainly have been writing for some time and be employing an accountant.

FINAL TIPS AND WORDS OF ENCOURAGEMENT

Persevere

Very few authors succeed right away. Most spend years before they strike lucky. And luck does sometimes come into it. I asked how long people had been writing before the first acceptance.

- 'About six months. But I'd served a ten-year "apprenticeship" in magazine stories.' (Susan Sallis)

- 'About eight months, ie as long as it took to write the first one.' (Matthew Kneale)

- 'About a year.' (Frederick Nolan)

- 'I got published fairly quickly – two years after starting from scratch.' (Margaret James)

- 'Four years.' (Joan Hessayon)

- 'Four years.' (Anita Burgh)

- 'Six years.' (Andrew Puckett)

- 'Six years seriously.' (Anne Melville)

- 'Seriously trying to be accepted, about twelve years.' (A. Hulme)

- 'I finished my first novel when I was seventeen. I then wrote four more, very properly unpublished, novels before the first Charles Paris was accepted when I was twenty-nine.' (Simon Brett).

◆ 'Eighteen years. All my efforts to get a publisher failed. When it happened it was complete chance – a meeting with an agent at a party.' (Sara Banerji)

The writers not yet published had all completed at least three manuscripts, and started several more.

Tips and advice

◆ 'Read the best before you try to write.' (Judith Murdoch)

◆ 'Be open to constructive criticism – no one is perfect and you can *always* learn. And never give up.' (Carole Blake)

◆ 'Persevere, understand that writing is a craft and the more you practise the better you will become. Be prepared to take advice from professional editors. Some promising authors cannot take advice and do not succeed for that reason.' (Judy Piatkus)

◆ 'A friend once told me: "Remember the value of competence. Forget genius – if you can deliver a piece of work that's on the right subject, and the right length, and meets its deadline and is delivered to the right publisher – then you're already ahead of eighty per cent of professional writers."' (Simon Brett)

◆ 'Persevere if you believe in yourself.' (Jane Morpeth)

◆ 'If a busy editor has taken time to write a critique (with a rejection slip) it's because she thinks there's something there worth criticising. If she asks to see some more work, send some.' (Ann Hulme)

- 'Sometimes you'll have bad days and will think you'll be writing rubbish. Often you'll be right. But keep going and you may just end up with something that's grown and fused into something far better than you would ever have believed on those bad days.' (Matthew Kneale)

- 'Keep writing – keep launching those messages in bottles, be patient, your time will come, even if it's 200 years in the future when they discover your genius, and always read.' (Philip Pullman)

- 'Publishers are always looking for the writer with a new idea or a fresh voice. Don't be afraid to follow your own star – it's always better than following someone else's.' (Frederick Nolan)

- 'Don't give up. Cultivate a sense of humour. Accept that life is Not Fair for most people, and Especially Not Fair for writers.' (Andrew Puckett)

- 'Most important, relax and enjoy writing or else it will show.' (Anita Burgh)

DISCUSSION POINTS

1. Look at some book jackets and decide which are most effective, and why.

2. What sort of personal publicity do you feel able to do?

3. How well do you understand contracts and taxation leaflets? Do you need professional help with these before you get into a muddle?

Appendix 1
Sources of Quotes

A few people have changed jobs since they answered the questionnaire. Their new positions, where known, are in brackets.

AGENTS

Carole Blake. Joint Managing Director, Blake Friedman, Literary, TV and Film Agency Ltd.

Barbara Levy. Sole Proprietor, Barbara Levy Literary Agency.

Laura Longrigg. Literary Agent, Jennifer Kavanah Agency. (MBA Literary Agency).

Dorothy Lumley. Proprietor, Dorian Literary Agency.

Sarah Molloy. Director, A. M. Heath & Co Ltd.

Judith Murdoch. Proprietor, Judith Murdoch Literary Agency.

Caroline Sheldon. Proprietor, Caroline Sheldon Literary Agency.

Bob Tanner. Managing Director, International Scripts.

BOOKSELLERS

Richard Carr. Customer Service Manager, WH Smith's, High Wycombe.

Ralph James. Director, James Redshaw Ltd, Lichfield.

Brian Pattinson. Owner of several bookshops in Oxfordshire.

EDITORS

Diane Allen. Rights and Acquisitions Manager, Magna Large Print Books.

Jill Black. Former Editorial Director, The Bodley Head. Administrator for the Georgette Heyer and the Catherine Cookson Prizes.

Luigi Bonomi. Editorial Director, Signet (Penguin Books Ltd). (Agent with Sheil and Land Associates.)

Barbara Boote. Editorial Director, Little, Brown and Company (UK) Ltd.

Beverley Cousins. Senior Editor, Macmillan Publishers Ltd.

Elizabeth Johnson. Senior Editor, Harlequin Mills and Boon Ltd, (now retired).

Michael Legat. Ex-Editorial Director, and author of several writers' guides.

Jane Morpeth. Publishing Director (Fiction), Headline.

Judy Piatkus. Managing Director, Piatkus Books.

Deborah Smith. Managing Editor, Severn House Publishers.

Richenda Todd. Senior Editor, Michael Joseph. (Freelance editor.)

LIBRARIANS

Anne Ambler. Oxfordshire.

Christine Budworth. District Librarian, Cannock.

Margaret Garfitt, Senior Library Assistant, Ludlow.

Tracy Long. Library Manager, Solihull.

Sue Richardson. Library Manager, Solihull.

Lynn Sanders. Library Supervisor, Walsall.

Mary Wilson. Holt Jackson Book Co.

NOVELISTS – PUBLISHED

Sara Banerji. Author of several highly acclaimed novels set in India.

Simon Brett. Radio and TV script writer, broadcaster, author of crime novels.

Anita Burgh. Best-selling author of both historical and modern books.

Joan Hessayon. Author of several historicals set in England and America.

Ann Hulme. Author of historicals as Ann Hulme, and more recently crime novels as Ann Granger.

Margaret James. Author of several novels. Columnist in *Writing* magazine, editor and ghost-writer for StorytrackS Agency.

Matthew Kneale. Runner-up for the Betty Trask Award, winner of both the Somerset Maugham Award and John Llewellyn Rhys Memorial Award. Won the Whitbread Book of the Year in 2000.

Anne Melville. Wrote under several pseudonyms, adult and children's fiction, and short stories. Winner (as Anne Betteridge) of the Romantic Novel of the Year Award (1967) with *The Truth Game*.

Haydn Middleton. Author of best-selling historical and fantasy novels.

Frederick Nolan. Novelist, script-writer, former reviewer and workshop leader.

Andrew Puckett. Has written several crime novels and teaches writing classes.

Philip Pullman. Author of novels for children and young adults, historical and fantasy. Has won many prizes, including being the first children's author to win the Whitbread.

Susan Sallis. Best-selling author of many family sagas.

Reay Tannahill. Winner of the Romantic Novel of the Year Award (1990) with *Passing Glory*, has also written acclaimed non-fiction books.

NOVELISTS — UNPUBLISHED

Diana Atkinson
Clare Knight
Zoë March

READERS

Joan Beard
Valerie Bennett
Mary Brackley
Nancy Brazier
Hanna Bridgeman
Jo Crocker
Anne Donnelly
Christine Evans
Molly Frearson
Carol Gough
Rosemary Guiver
Frances Hawkins
Susan Jones
Yvonne Morley
Sylvia Parker
Judy Phillips
Jill Rundle

REVIEWERS

Rebecca Abrams. Freelance reviewer of both fiction and non-fiction for *The Guardian*, also author of non-fiction books, and journalist.

Sarah Broadhurst. Freelance reviewer for *The Bookseller*, several regional papers, *Woman's Journal* and radio.

F. E. Pardoe. Retired as Head of Communication Studies at Birmingham Polytechnic (now the University of Central England). Reviewed mainly crime for *The Birmingham Post*.

Appendix 2
List of UK Publishers

LIST OF UK PUBLISHERS

This is by no means a comprehensive list, but includes the major publishers of fiction. Search the latest Yearbooks for details which may have changed since this book was published, and for the smaller, often more specialised publishers, who may, for example, publish Welsh language or Scottish interest novels. These publishers pay royalties, but some of the smaller ones may ask for a contribution towards production costs, or share profits. Check carefully the terms they offer.

KEY

A – adventure, thrillers   C – crime, mystery, suspense
G – general   H – historical
L – literary   R – romantic
S – science fiction, fantasy   O – other

PUBLISHERS

Allison & Busby (**C,G,O**) Suite 111, Bon Marche Centre, 241 Ferndale Road, London SW9 8BJ. Tel: (020) 7738 7883. Fax: (020) 7733 4244. Email: *all@allisonbusby.co.uk*

Black and White Publishing Ltd (**G**) 99 Giles Street, Edinburgh EH6 6BZ. Tel: (0131) 625 4500. Fax: (0131) 625 4501. Email: *mail@blackandwhitepublishing.com*

Black Ace Books (**G**) PO Box 6557, Forfar DD8 2YS. Tel: (01307) 465096. Fax: (01307) 465494.

Bloomsbury (**A,C,G,L**) 38 Soho Square, London W1D 3HB. Tel: (020) 7494 2111. Fax: (020) 7434 0151.

The Book Guild Ltd (**G**) Temple House, High Street, Lewes, East Sussex BN7 2LU. Tel: (01273) 472534. Fax: (01273) 476472. Email: *info@bookguild.co.uk*

Marion Boyars Publishers Ltd (**G,H,L,O**) 24 Lacy Road, London SW15 1NL. Tel: (020) 8788 9522. Fax: (020) 8789 8122. Email: *rebecca@marion.boyers.co.uk*

Calder Publications Ltd (**L**) 51 The Cut, London SE1 8LF. Tel: (020) 7633 0599. Email: *info@calderpublications.com*

Canongate Books Ltd (**G,H,L**) 14 High Street, Edinburgh EH1 1TE. Tel: (0131) 557 5111. Fax: (0131) 557 5211. Email: *info@canongate.co.uk*

Constable & Robinson Ltd (**C,G,H,L,S**) 3 The Lanchesters, 162 Fulham Palace Road, London W6 9ER. Tel: (020) 8741 3663. Fax: (020) 8748 7562. Email: *enquiries@constablerobinson.com*

Dedalus Ltd (**O,L**) Langford Lodge, St Judith's Lane, Sawtry, Cambs PE17 5XE. Tel/Fax: (01487) 832 382. Email: *info@dedalus.com*

Gerald Duckworth & Co. Ltd (**G**) First Floor, 90/93 Cowcross Street, London EC1M 6BF. Tel: (020) 7490 7300. Fax: (020) 7490 0080. Email: *info@duckworth-publishers.co.uk*

Faber & Faber Ltd (**C,G,L,O**) 3 Queen Square, London WC1N 3AU. Tel: (020) 7465 0054. Fax: (020) 7465 0034.

Granta Books (**L**) 2/3 Hanover Yard, Noel Road, London N1 8BE. Tel: (020) 7704 9776. Fax: (020) 7354 3469.

Robert Hale Ltd (**G,H,R,O**) Clerkenwell House, 45–47 Clerkenwell Green, London EC1R 0HT. Tel: (020) 7251 2661. Fax: (020) 7490 4958. Email: *enquiries@halebooks.com*

Harlequin Mills & Boon, Eton House, 18–24 Paradise Road, Richmond, Surrey TW9 1SR. Tel: (020) 8288 2800. Fax: (020) 8288 2899.

HarperCollins (**A,C,G,H,L,R,S**) (Collins – **C**, Flamingo – **L**) 77–85 Fulham Palace Road, Hammersmith, London W6 8JB. Tel: (020) 8741 7070. Fax: (020) 8307 4440.

Hodder Headline (**A,C,G,H,L,S,R**) (Coronet – **A,C,R,S**, Delta – **O**, Liaison **O**, New English Library – **A,C,S**, Sceptre – **A,C,G,H,L**) 338 Euston Road, London, NW1 3BH. Tel: (020) 7873 6000. Fax: (020) 7873 6024.

Macmillan Publishers Ltd (**C,G,L,R**) (Pan – **A,C,G,H,L,R,S**, Picador – **L**) The Macmillan Building, 4 Crinian Street, London N1 9XW. Tel: (020) 7833 4000. Fax: (020) 7843 4640.

The Orion Publishing Group Ltd (**A,C,G,H,L,R,S**) (Chapman – **O**, Millenium – **S**, Phoenix House – **L**) Orion House, 5 Upper St Martin's Lane, London WC2H 9EA. Tel: (020) 7240 3444. Fax: (020) 7240 4822.

Penguin UK (Hamish Hamilton – **C,G,L,O**, Viking – **C,G,L**, Michael Joseph – **A,C,H,R**) 80 Strand, London WC2R 0RL. Tel: (020) 7010 3000. Fax: (020) 7010 6060.

Piatkus Books (**A,C,G,H,R**) 5 Windmill Street, London W1T 2JA. Tel: (020) 7631 0710. Fax: (020) 7436 7137. Email: *info@piatkus.co.uk*

Quartet Books Ltd (**G**) 27 Goodge Street, London W1T 2LD. Tel: (020) 7636 3992. Fax: (020) 7637 1866.

Random House Group Ltd (**A,C,G,H,L,R,S**) (Arrow – **C,S**, Cape – **G,H,L**, Chatto – **A,C,G,L**, Century – **G,L,R**, Hutchinson – **A,C,G,H,L**, Legend – **S**) 20 Vauxhall Bridge Road, London SW1V 2SA. Tel: (020) 7840 8400. Fax: (020) 7233 6058. Email: *enquiries@randomhouse.co.uk*

Serpent's Tail (**C,G,L,O**) 4 Blackstock Mews, London N4 2BT. Tel: (020) 7354 1949. Fax: (020) 7704 6467. Email: *info@serpentstail.com*

Severn House Publishers (**A,C,R,S**) 9–15 High Street, Sutton, Surrey SM1 1DF. Tel: (020) 8770 3930. Fax: (020) 8770 3850. Email: *info@severnhouse.com*

Simon & Schuster (**A,G,H**) (Pocket Books – **G**) Africa House, 64–78 Kingsway, London WC2B 6AH. Tel: (020) 7316 1900. Fax: (020) 7316 0333.

Souvenir Press Ltd (**A,C,G,H,L**) 43 Great Russell Street, London WC1B 3PA. Tel: (020) 7580 9307/8 and 7637 5711/2/3. Fax: (020) 7580 5064. Email: *souvenirpress@ukon-line.co.uk*

Time Warner Books (**A,C,G,H,R,S**) (Abacus – **L**, Orbit – **S**, Warner – **A,C,G,H,O,R**). Tel: (020) 7911 8000. Fax: (020) 7911 8100. Email: *uk@twbg.co.uk*

Transita (**G**) 3 Newtec Place, Magdalen Road, Oxford OX4 1RE. Tel: (01865) 204 393. Fax: (01865) 248 780. Email: *info@transita.co.uk*

Transworld Publishers Ltd (Bantam – **A,C,G,H,L,R,S,O**, Black Swan – **A,C,G,H,L,R,S**, Corgi – **A,C,G,L,R,S,O**, Doubleday – **A,G,H,L,R**) 61–63 Uxbridge Road, London W5 5SA. Tel: (020) 8579 2652. Fax: (020) 8579 5479. Email: *info@trans-world-publishers.co.uk*

Virgin Books Ltd (Black Lace – **O**, Nexus – **O**, Virgin Worlds. **S**) Thames Wharf Studios, Rainville Road, London W6 9HT. Tel: (020) 7386 3300. Fax: (020) 7386 3360. Email: *info@virgin-book.co.uk*

The Women's Press (**A,L,S,O**) 27 Goodge Street, London W1T 8LD Tel: (020) 7436 3992 Fax: (020) 7637 1866.

ELECTRONIC PUBLISHERS

Most of these are based in the USA. Some pay royalties. Some ask the author for a fee to display the novel online. Their email addresses and Internet sites are listed in Appendix 3.

Appendix 3
Internet Sites

INTERNET SERVICE PROVIDERS

You will need one before you can access the Internet, but you can now try it out first in Cyber cafés and many libraries. *www.herbison.com* gives lists and information.

The following are some of the big ISPs. Some charge, others are free apart from phone costs.

www.uk.aol.com
www.compuserve.co.uk
www.btinternet.com
www.clara.net
www.demon.net
www.wanadoo.co.uk
www.global.net.uk
www.uk.msn.com
www.virgin.net
www.dial.pipex.com
www.ukonline.co.uk
www.talk21.com
www.btopenworld.com
www.supanet.com
www.tesco.net
www.netscape.net
www.lineone.net

For a separate email address you can try *hotmail.msn.co.uk*
To locate websites you need to use a search engine, such as one of the following, or a search directory, the final two.

www.albany.net/allinone is a directory of directories and search engines. The other URLs are all *www.(name).com search altavista dogpile* (searches several simultaneously) *excite hotbot infoseek lycos opentext webcrawler yahoo god.uk/*

SOFTWARE

There are programs available for free or a trial run.

www.download.com library of software
www.freewarenow.com software
www.jumbo.com software
www.ferretsoft.com/netferret/products.html can search several
  engines quickly

BOOKSHOPS

Many sell not only books, but tapes, videos, CDs, etc.

www.bookweb.org/directory links to many bookstores
www.ablebooks.co.uk booksearch
www.alibris.com
www.amazon.com
www.amazon.co.uk
www.BarnesandNoble.com
www.bibliofind.com lists of rare books
www.bol.com
www.promo.net/pg This site is attempting to provide out of
  copyright classics online.
www.waterstones.co.uk
www.bookshop.co.uk
www.kingbooks.com

ENCYCLOPAEDIAS AND DICTIONARIES

There are many available online, and as CDs.

www.britannica.com

www.clever.net/cam/encyclopedia.html has a classification of
   resources on the net
www.dictionaryofslang.co.uk
www.itools.com has links
www.oed.com Oxford English Dictionary
www.yourdictionary.com 230 languages

GENERAL RESEARCH

This is a random list of a few sites I have found useful, many of
them having links to further information.

www.agentsassoc.co.uk Professional association for agents with
   list of current members
www.bartleby.com online reference books
www.bbc.co.uk
www.bibliomania.com
www.booktrust.org.uk
www.thebookseller.com
www.publishingnews.com
www.writersdigest.com
www.writers-free-reference.com
www.script-o-rama.com index of movie and TV scripts available
   on Internet
www.pro.gov.uk Public Records Office
www.lawrights.co.uk factsheets on UK legal matters
www.cr-law.co.uk legal information
www.patient.co.uk medicine in the UK
www.nil.nih.gov National Library of Medicine
www.ecola.com links to online magazines, by subject
www.multimap.com local street maps and details
www.numberway.com has links to telephone directories round
   the world

LIBRARIES

Many major libraries, including university ones, are online. They can guide you to resources. *ac* or *edu* in the URL indicates university or college.

www.a2a.org.uk database of UK archive catalogues
www.bl.uk British Library
www.lib.ox.ac.uk links you to Oxford libraries
www.statistics.gov.uk Office for National Statistics

ADVICE, ONLINE COURSES, INFORMATION AND CONTACTS WITH OTHER WRITERS

(Many of these sites are USA based, but they still have lots of useful information for authors outside the USA. See also websites in the addresses list of UK organisations. You may need to register for some sites or pay for information.)

www.nec.ac.uk National Extension College Courses
www.ucas.com details of courses
www.absolutewrite.com
www.author.co.uk
www.author-network.com
www.authorhouse.co.uk helps self-publishers
www.bloomsburymagazine.com
www.bol.com news for the book trade
www.noveladvice.com has tips as well as information on courses
www.readytowrite.com
www.storytracks.net tips and critique service
www.harrybowlingprize.net details of bi-annual prize for novels
    set in London
www.hollylisle.com
www.charlottedillon.com
www.thecwa.com Crime Writers' Association
www.murdersquad.org seven northern UK crime writers
www.rna-uk.org Romantic Novelists' Association

www.societyofauthors.org
www.theslot.com copy-editor's guide
www.grammarqueen.com
www.eclectics.com/writing.html
www.authorlink.com
www.writerswrite.com
aol and compuserve have sites for subscribers only
www.horrornet.net horror and suspense
www.rwanational.com Romance Writers of America
www.sfwa.org Science Fiction and Fantasy Writers of America
www.scifiweekly.com magazine
www.writers.net
www.writersnet.org.uk
www.wordup.co.uk
www.writersbbs.com sponsors chats and discussion forums
www.writers.com
www.writing-world.com
www.literatureawards.com.

SELF PROMOTION

You can have your own sites, and there are many sites and chat groups hosted by fans of writers too. The following are a small selection.

www.anitaburgh.com
www.marina-oliver.net the author of this book
www.elizabethchadwick.com who writes medieval historicals
www.lizfielding.com Liz Fielding who writes for Harlequin Mills and Boon
www.annajacobs.com saga writer
www.penny-jordan.com
For other links to members of the Romantic Novelists' Association go to *www.rna-uk.org*
www.lindseydavis.co.uk crime writer

For other links to members of the Crime Writers' Association go to *www.thecwa.co.uk*

www.dkoontz.com Dean Koontz

For links to other authors' websites go to *google.com* or *google.co.uk* and type the name

www.authorlink.com is an online repository to market work to agents

www.acwl.org American Crime Writers' League

PUBLISHERS

Most publishers have websites, and more are coming. URLs are in the *Yearbook* or *Handbook*, but below is a list of some major electronic publishers of fiction. Most are in America. Links to others are on some of the general information for writers sites above. One of the most useful sites is *http://my.coredcs.com/ ~mermaid/epubs.html*

Electronic publishers

As with conventional publishers, their terms differ, so check what you are being offered first. Some online publishers accept anything, and charge authors for displaying their work rather than acting as a publisher who selects appropriate scripts, takes the risk and markets the novel, often in paper as well as electronic format.

BeWrite Books email: *info@bewrite.net*
    Website: *www.bewrite.net*
Claritybooks.com email: *editor@claritybooks.com*
    Website: *claritybooks.com*
Deunant Books email: *mail@deunantbooks.com*
    Website: *www.deunantbooks.com*
Dreams Unlimited email: *info@dreams-unlimited.com*
    Website: *www.dreams-unlimited.com*
Hard Shell Word Factory email: *books@hardshell.com*
    Website: *www.eclectics.com* or *www.hardshell.com*

Instread email: *submit@instread.com*
   Website: *www.instread.com*
New Concepts Press email: *ncp@newconceptspublishing.com*
   Website: *www.newconceptspublishing.com*
Online Originals Priory Cottage, Wordsworth Place, London.
   NW5 4HG. Tel: (020) 7267 4244.
   Email: *editor@onlineoriginals.com*
   Website: *www.onlineoriginals.com*
Warehouse publishing guidelines from
   authorswanted@myreply.com
A good list, mainly of USA electronic publishers, is at
   www.maryzwolf.com

Publishing houses' sites

These are conventional paper publishers. With most of the names it is obvious which publisher owns the site.

www.bookport.com/welcome/9550 Internet Book Fair, and Map
   to online book resources
www.bookfair.com/welcome/bookfair/bphome directory of publishers' sites worldwide
www.bookwire.com/index.html Publishers's Weekly guide to
   publishers' websites
www.lights.com/publisher index of publishers worldwide
publisher@internet.handbooks.co.uk
www.allisonandbusby.com
www.bbcworldwide.com
www.blackacebooks.com
www.bloomsburymagazine.com
www.booksattransworld.co.uk
www.marionboyars.co.uk
www.calderpublications.com
www.cambridge.org Cambridge University Press
www.canongate.net

www.constablerobinson.com
www.ducknet.co.uk
www.faber.co.uk
www.granta.com
www.guinnessworldrecords.com
www.eharlequin.com
www.millsandboon.co.uk
www.harpercollins.com
www.granta.com
www.halebooks.com
www.hodderheadline.co.uk
www.helicon.co.uk
www.howtobooks.co.uk
www.macmillan.com
www.oup.com Oxford University Press
www.penguin.co.uk
www.piatkus.co.uk
www.randomhouse.co.uk
www.reedelsevier.com
www.routledge.com
www.serpentstail.com
www.severnhouse.com
www.simonsays.co.uk Simon & Schuster site with discussions, etc
www.twgb.co.uk Time Warner Books
www.transita.co.uk
www.virginbooks.com
www.the-womens-press.com

Glossary

Acceptance. An offer to publish the manuscript.

Advance. Money given to an author by a publisher on signing a contract to write a book and/or on delivery of script and publication of that book.

Agent. A person or company that acts on an author's behalf, selling the author's work and negotiating fees. Agents take a percentage of authors' earnings.

aka. also known as.

Allowable expenses. Those expenses on machinery, equipment and essential requirements an author has in order to work, which can be offset against income before income tax is charged.

Angle. The way something is shown, which might be serious or funny, mysterious or straightforward, or the point of view it is written from.

Antagonist. Character who is opposed to the protagonist.

Auctions. An agent will invite several publishers to bid for a script by a certain deadline. This happens with a few very important works.

Blockbuster. A large book of fiction, often aimed at the holiday market.

Blog. A diary published on the Internet.

Blurb. A summary of the book which is printed on the back cover or on the first page of a book, and designed to attract readers.

Book jacket. The outer cover of the book, usually with an illustration.

Bookmarks. List of favourite websites for quick access.

Bulletin boards. A notice board on the Internet for posting messages.

Cast. The characters in your novel.

Category fiction. Books/fiction of a particular type, eg romance or science fiction, which are published as a regular series and have similarities within the series such as length, style and conventions.

CDs. Compact disks, on which vast amounts of data, including audio and video, can be stored electronically.

Characters. The people who feature in your novel.

Chat groups. Where it is possible to 'talk' online with other people by typing in comments, etc. Many are specialist interest groups.

Cliffhanger. An exciting, unresolved situation at the end of a scene or chapter.

Communities. Interest groups on the Internet with facilities for activities such as chat, displaying work and accessing reference material.

Competition. Where a prize is given for a novel, either published or in script form.

Conflict. Some disagreement, aims which are incompatible.

Contents. The list at the start of a book/magazine which lists the subjects covered and/or chapter headings and page numbers.

Continuity. Keeping details consistent from scene to scene.

Contract. The terms agreed by author and publisher, covering such matters as payment, publication, ownership of second rights and proportions of earnings allocated under these.

Convention. A large gathering usually including fans and readers as well as writers.

Copy. A piece of writing sent to a publisher.

Copy-editing. Checking details and altering a writer's work for the house style of the publisher.

Copyright. The legal rights an author/publisher has over their work, so that no one can copy all or part of the work without the author's or publisher's permission.

Courses. Lectures and exercises, by post or in person, on the art and various aspects of writing.

Cover sheet. The first page of a manuscript giving title, author, author's address and telephone number, and wordage.

Creative writing classes/courses. Often run by local authorities or educational institutions, they may be weekly sessions, day or weekend or longer.

Criticism. A detailed appraisal of a piece of writing.

Critique group. A group of writers who meet to criticise (hopefully constructively) others' work. Groups usually comprise amateur writers, but published writers do join.

Deadline. The date by which a writer aims to complete or submit a script.

Description. Portraying scenes in words.

Deus ex machina. Literally the 'God from the machine', an unexpected event which solves an apparently impossible situation.

Dialect. The words peculiar to one region or area of a country.

Dialogue. Conversation, or the words spoken by characters.

Disk. A device for storing computer programs and data.

Double spacing. Lines typed to give approximately three lines per inch on a manuscript (single spacing gives six).

Draft. A version of a manuscript, usually the first thoughts.

Editing. Checking on accuracy, consistency, relevance, structure, and generally preparing a piece of writing for publication.

Edition. A book may be published in different formats, each one is a separate edition.

Editor. The person who commissions writers for books/articles/ plays and who sees the project through to the final printing and distribution.

Electronic reader. A small battery-operated machine which can store large amounts of text, such as several books, and which can be read independently.

Electronic rights. The author's copyright over reproduction of his work in electronic form, such as on the Internet.

Email. Electronic mail, a method of communicating with others via the Internet. Each user world-wide has a unique address.

Enquiry letter. Letter to the editor outlining what an author has written, how long it is and why it might be of interest to the publisher.

Exposition. An explanation of events, feelings or actions in the novel.

FAQS. Frequently asked questions, often posted on websites or newsgroups.

Flashback. Portrayal of a scene from the past as if it is taking place now.

Flash forward. Putting in a scene from the future, or a brief foretelling of what is still to come.

Font. A style and size of type, eg *italic* 10.

Foreshadowing. Hinting, or laying down the clues for something which is to happen later in the book.

Genre. A type of book, eg crime, fantasy, historical, literary, romantic, saga, science fiction, western.

Grammar. Rules applying to words and their relationships to one another.

Hardback. Where the cover of the book is stiff.

Hard copy. Paper print-out of text as opposed to a display on a computer screen.

Hook. The means by which a writer obtains the reader's attention and interest.

Hot link. Or hyperlink, appears on web pages as a short cut to other web pages, and a mouse-click transfers you directly to the other page.

House style. Every publisher/magazine will have certain ways of writing things, for example standardising on spellings such as the use of 'ise' instead of 'ize' at the end of words like criticise.

HTML. HyperText Mark-up Language is a special programming language which is used for designing web pages.

Internet. A link, via a computer and telephone, to other computers for correspondence, information, or exchange of ideas.

ISPs. Internet service providers are companies which provide, amongst other services, access to the Internet.

Jeopardy. A danger or peril which threatens characters. A sub-genre of romantic fiction is the 'woman in jeopardy'.

Large print. Editions of a book in a big typeface, intended to make reading easier for people with eyesight problems.

Layout. The way the writing is set out on the page, with margins, line spacing, headings.

Libel. A false, damaging statement published in permanent form.

Link. See **hot link**.

Manuscript/script/typescript. An author's typed/word processed piece of work.

Market. Any place where a writer's work may be sold.

Modifiers. Words which qualify, change or restrict others.

Moral rights. The rights of 'paternity', *ie* having one's authorship recognised, and of integrity, *ie* not having the work changed in a 'derogatory' manner. These rights have to be asserted in writing by the author.

Multiple submissions. Sending work to more than one publisher at a time.

Narrative. The telling of a story.

Networking. Forming connections with other people.

Newsgroups. Similar to **bulletin boards**, special interest groups for posting messages and communication.

Online. A connection to another computer or a service.

Outline. A very brief summary of a piece of work.

Pace. The speed of progress, whether fast or slow, smooth or jerky, of a piece of writing.

Padding. Inserting irrelevant detail.

Page proofs. Typeset manuscripts in page layout.

Paperback. A book the cover of which is flexible card or thick paper.

Partials. Part of a book which the publisher likes to see, in order to judge whether to read the rest with a view to publication. It is normally the first three chapters or fifty pages.

Phonetics. Writing sounds, especially of regional or foreign accents, using one symbol for each sound rather than the conventional spelling. Miss could be mees or mizz.

Plagiarism. Deliberately to copy another writer's ideas such as plot and characters and use them as your own.

Plot. A series of happenings connected by cause and effect.

Polishing. Checking a manuscript to make final changes and corrections.

Presentation. The way in which a manuscript is shown to an editor.

Printer. 1) The machine which produces, on paper, documents stored in a computer. There are different types using different processes. 2) The person or firm which typesets books and produces copies.

Program. The system by which a computer receives and deals with data.

Proofreading. Final check of galleys or page proofs for typos, spelling mistakes, missing text and so on.

Proofs. Typeset article/book which is corrected for printing.

Proof marks. The symbols used to indicate changes needed.

Proposal. Detailed outline of a project, together with a synopsis.

Protagonist. One of the leading characters.

Pseudonym. A name used by an author which is not his own, a pen name.

Publicity. Spreading information by various means, the media or personally.

Public Lending Right. Money an author gets each time her book is borrowed from a library. The author must register each new edition on publication or before the end of June each year to receive payment the following February.

Publisher's reader. Someone who reads and assesses manuscripts, and passes on suitable ones for final editorial decision on buying.

Pulping. When books/magazines are sent back to the publisher/distributor because they are not bought, some are destroyed by reducing them to pulp which then goes to make paper.

Punctuation. Symbols used to make the written words clear and understandable.

Rejections. When an agent or publisher declines to handle or buy a manuscript. There are many reasons for rejection apart from the quality of the work.

Remainders. The books that are left after sales have fallen off are remaindered – offered to the author at a cheap rate and to cheap book shops.

Research. Discovering and verifying facts which may be used in or as background for the novel.

Review. A report, usually in the media, assessing a book.

Revising. Checking a piece of writing and making changes in it, improving it, and making sure the facts are accurate.

Rewriting. Changing a piece of writing, sometimes radically, sometimes with only minor alterations.

Rights. Legal rights of an author in terms of the sale of a piece of work.

Royalties. A percentage of the selling price of a book that goes to the author after publication, based on the numbers sold or the monies received.

Search directory. A device for finding information on the Internet, organised on a 'tree and branch' system.

Search engine. Another Internet searching device, which will locate websites identified by a phrase or word.

Second rights. Editions of a book or article after the first publication, eg paperback, large print, translation, syndication, extracts, anthologies, adaptations for radio or TV or film.

Shape. The form and pattern of the novel

Slush pile. The term used for unsolicited manuscripts received.

Softback. See paperback.

Software. Programs for computers.

Solicited script. Work an editor has asked to see.

Spellchecker. Computer spelling tool, which can highlight errors and often suggest alternative words.

Spread. Two pages facing one another in a book or magazine.

Submissions. The manuscripts sent to editors for consideration, in the hope of acceptance.

Subplot. A minor, subsidiary plot in a novel.

Summary. A three- or four-line outline of what a piece of writing is all about.

Suspense. Uncertainty about the outcome.

Synonym. A word with the same or a similar meaning as another word.

Synopsis. A detailed summary of a novel, giving all important facts about the plot and characters.

Target. Aim.

Theme. A subject of a novel, often an abstract quality.

Thesaurus. A book which gives alternative words of the same or similar meaning, and where concepts are grouped.

Title page. Cover sheet of manuscript.

Trade paperback. A book with a flexible cover, but usually of a larger format and higher price than the conventional paperback.

Turning point. A crisis or time when some decision is made or resolution achieved.

Typeface. The style of the typed characters. There are many different typefaces, publishers will use different ones for different projects.

Typesetting. Putting a piece of writing into the typeface, size and in the appropriate space that the publisher uses.

Typos. Typing errors on the manuscript or galleys.

Unsolicited. Work sent on spec to an agent or editor.

URL. (**uniform resource locator**). The address of a website.

VAT. Value Added Tax, imposed on almost all purchases, which can be reclaimed by persons registered under the scheme.

Viewpoint. The character through whose eyes the action is seen or described.

Voice. The particular individual style of a writer.

Website. Pages set up by individuals, organisations and companies to advertise, impart information, or sell items.

White space. The empty space at the ends of short lines and chapters.

Wordage. The approximate number of words in a manuscript, calculated by multiplying the average number per line by the lines in a page and the total pages.

Word processing. Using a computer in order to type work, and then being able to manipulate the information by inserting, deleting, moving text, changing the layout and many more processes.

World Wide Web. The system of websites connected by the Internet.

Writer's block. When a writer cannot continue, through lack of ideas or motivation, exhaustion, or psychological difficulties.

Yearbook. A reference book published annually, such as *The Writers' and Artists' Yearbook* or *The Writers' Handbook*.

Useful Addresses

WRITING COURSES

Online courses
There are many courses available, at all levels, on the Internet. See Appendix 3.

Correspondence colleges
Correspondence colleges provide both general and specific courses.

The London School of Journalism, 126 Shireland Road, London W9 2BT. Tel: (020) 7432 7777. Fax: (020) 7432 8141. Email: *info@lsjournalism.com*
Website: *www.home-study.com*

National Extension College, Michael Young Centre, Purbeck Road, Cambridge CB2 2HN. Tel: (01223) 400 350. Fax: (01223) 400 325.

Real Writers, PO Box 170, Chesterfield, Derbyshire S40 1FE. Tel: 01246 238 492. Email: *info@real-wrtrs.com*
Website: *www.real-writers.com*

The Writer's Bureau, Sevendale House, 7 Dale Street, Manchester M1 1JB. Tel: (0161) 228 2362. Fax: (0161) 236 9440. Email: *studentservices@writersbureau.com*
Website: *www.writersbureau.com*

Writers News Home Study Division, PO Box 4, Nairn IV12 4HU. Tel: (0113) 200 2917.
Email: *rachel.betterby@writersnews.co.uk*
Website: *www.writersnews.co.uk*

Short courses

Creative writing short courses, usually residential, are held in many places, including the following venues. As programmes change every year, contact the course organisers for details.

Alston Hall, Alston Lane, Longridge, Preston PR3 3BP. Tel: (01772) 784 661. Fax: (01772) 785 835.
   Email: *alstonhall@ed.lancscc.gov.org*
   Website: *www.alstonhall.com*
The Arvon Foundation, 2nd Floor, 42A Buckingham Palace Road, London SW1W 0RE. Tel: (020) 7931 7611. Fax: (020) 7963 0961.
The Arvon Foundation, Lumb Bank, Heptonstall, Hebden Bridge, West Yorks HX7 6DF. Tel/Fax: (01422) 843 714.
   Email: *l-bank@arvonfoundation.org*
   Website: *www.arvonfoundation.org*
The Arvon Foundation, Moniack Mhor, Teavarran, Kiltarlity, Beauly, Inverness-shire IV4 7HT. Tel: (01463) 741675. Email: *m-mhor@arvonfoundation.org*
The Arvon Foundation, Totleigh Barton, Sheepwash, Beaworthy, Devon EX21 5NS. Tel: (01409) 231 338. Fax: (01409) 231144. Email: *t-barton@arvonfoundation.org*
Belfast Queen's University, Institute of Lifelong Learning, Belfast BT7 1NN. Tel: (028) 9097 3323. Fax: (028) 9097 1084. Email: *ill@qub.ac.uk* Website: *www.qub.ac.uk/ill*
Birmingham University Centre for Lifelong Learning, Selly Oak, Birmingham B29 2TT 6LL. Tel: (0121) 41 3413. Fax: (0121) 414 5619. Email: *e.mbrackkanpayne@bham.ac.uk*
The City Literary Institute, Keeley Street, Covent Garden, London WC2B 4BA. Tel: (020) 7492 2652. Fax: (020) 7492 8256. Email: *humanities@citylit.ac.uk*
City University, Northampton Square, London EC1V 0HB. Tel: (020) 7040 8268. Fax: (020) 7040 8256. Email: *conted@city.ac.uk* Website: *www.city.ac.uk/conted*

Dingle Writing Courses Ltd, Ballintlea, Ventry, Co. Kerry, Republic of Ireland. Tel/Fax: (00353) 59815.
Email: *info@dinglewritingcourses.ie*
Website: *www.dinglewritingcourses.ie*

Dundee University, Institute for Education and Lifelong Learning, Nethergate, Dundee DD1 4HN. Tel: (01382) 344 809. Fax: (01382) 221 057. Email: *s.z.norrie@dundee.ac.uk*
Website: *www.dundee.ac.uk/learning*

The Earnley Concourse, Earnley, Chichester, Sussex PO20 7JL. Tel: (01243) 670 392. Fax: (01243) 670 832. Email: *info@earnley.co.uk* Website: *www.earnley.co.uk*

Edinburgh University Office of Lifelong Learning, 11 Buccleuch Place, Edinburgh EH8 9LW. Tel: (0131) 650 4400. Fax: (0131) 667 6097. Email: *oll@ed.ac.uk*
Website: *www.cce.ed.co.uk/*

Glasgow University, Department of Adult and Continuing Education, 11 Eldon Street, Glasgow G3 6NH. Tel: (0141) 330 1835/1829. Fax: (0141) 330 1821.
Email: *enquiries@aca.gla.ac.uk* Website: *www.gla.ac.uk*

Higham Hall College, Bassenthwaite Lake, Cockermouth, Cumbria CA13 9SH. Tel: (01768) 776276. Fax: (01768) 776013. Email: *admin@highamhall.com*
Website: *www.highamhall.com*

Keele University, Centre for Continuing and Professional Education, Keele University (Freepost ST1666) Newcastle under Lyme, Staffordshire ST5 5BG. Tel: (01782) 583436.

Knuston Hall Residential College, Irchester, Wellingborough, Northamptonshire NN9 7EU. Tel: (01933) 312104. Fax: (01933) 357596. Email: *enquiries@knustonhall.org.uk*
Website: *www.knustonhall.org.uk*

Lancaster University English and Creative Writing, Bowland College, Bailrigg, Lancaster LA1 4YN. Tel: (01524) 594169. Fax: (01524) 594 247. Email: *L.kellett@lancaster.ac.uk*

Leicester Adult Education College, Writing School, Wellington Street, Leicester LE1 6HL. Tel: (0116) 233 4343. Fax: (0116) 233 4344. Email: *vm1@leicester-adult-ed.ac.uk* Website: *www.leicester-adult-ed.ac.uk*

Liverpool University, Centre for Continuing Education, 126 Mount Pleasant, Liverpool L69 3GR. Tel: (0151) 794 6900. Fax: (0151) 794 2544. Email: *conted@liverpool.ac.uk* Website: *www.liv.ac.uk*

Marlborough College, Marlborough, Wiltshire SN8 1PA. Tel: (01672) 892388/9. Fax: (01672) 892476. Email: *summer.school@marlboroughcollege.wilts.sch.uk*

Missenden Abbey, Great Missenden, Bucks HP16 0BD. Tel: (0845) 045 4040 Fax: (01755) 783 756. Email: *adultlearningchil@buckscc.gov.org*

Nottingham Trent University, Clifton Lane, Nottingham NG8 8NS. Tel: (0115) 848 6677. Fax: (0115) 848 6632. Email: *hum.postgrad@ntu.ac.uk*

Reading University School of Continuing Education, London Road, Reading, Berkshire RG1 5AQ. Tel: (0118) 378 8347. Email: *Cont-ed@reading.ac.uk*

University of Oxford Department of Continuing Education, Rewley House, 1 Wellingon Square, Oxford OX1 2JA. Tel: (01865) 280 356. Fax: (01865) 270 309. Email: *pp@conted.ox.ac.uk*

Sheffield Hallam University, Collegiate Crescent, Sheffield S10 2BP. Tel: (0114) 225 2543. Fax: (0114) 225 2430. Email: *fdsenenquiries@shu.ac.uk* Website: *www.shu.ac.uk*

Sheffield University Institute of Lifelong Learning, 196–198 West Street, Sheffield S1 4ET. Tel: (0114) 222 7000. Fax: (0114) 222 7001. Website: *shef.ac.uk/till*

Surrey University Adult and Continuing Education, Guildford, Surrey GU2 5XH. Tel: (01483) 68315 Fax: (01483) 686 191. Email: *ace@surrey.ac.uk* Website: *www.surrey.ac.uk*

Swanwick Writers' Summer School, at The Hayes Conference Centre, Nr Alfreton, Derbyshire.
Email: *jean.sutton@lineone.net*

The Talesin Trust, T Newydd, Llanystumdwy, Cricieth, Gwynedd LL52 0LW. Tel: (01766) 522 811. Fax: (01766) 523 095. Email: *post@tynewydd.org*

Urchfont Manor College, Urchfont, Nr Devizes, Wiltshire SN10 4RG. Tel: (01380) 840 495. Fax: (01380) 840 005.

Warwick University, Open Studies, Centre for Lifelong Learning, Coventry, Warwickshire CV4 7AL. Tel: (024) 7652 8286. Email: *k.rainsley@warwick.ac.uk*

Winchester, Annual Writers' Conference, Chinook, Southdown Road, Winchester, Hampshire SO21 2BY. Tel: (01962) 827056. Email: *barbara.large@writers-conference.com* Website: *www.winchester.ac.uk*

Workers Educational Association, Area offices (details in *The Writer's Handbook* or local telephone directories) have lists of courses locally.

Higher education and professional courses

Many of the above colleges also offer full time and degree courses (BA, MA, PhD and Media Studies). Lists of the courses run by universities and other specialist bodies can be found in *The Writers' and Artists' Yearbook*.

PROFESSIONAL ASSOCIATIONS

Once you are published there are many specialist associations. Contact addresses change frequently, so check the latest yearbooks.

* Associations that are open to unpublished writers or readers.

Academi is the National Society of Welsh Writers. 3rd Floor, Mount Stuart House, Mount Stuart Square, Cardiff CF1

6DQ. Tel: (029) 2047 2266. Fax: (029) 2049 2930. Email: *post@academi.org* Website *dspace.dial.pipex.com/academi*

*The British Science Fiction Association Ltd, 1 Long Row Close, Everden, Daventry, Northants NN11 3BE. Tel: (01327) 361661. Email: *bsfa@enterprise.net* For anyone interested in science fiction. Publishes *Matrix, Focus* and *Vector* magazines.

Crime Writers' Association, PO Box 273, Boreham Wood WD6 2XA. Email: *secretary@thecwa.co.uk*
Website: *www.thecwa.co.uk*

*Historical Novel Society, Richard Lee, Marine Cottage, The Strand, Starcross, Devon EX6 8NY. Tel: (01626) 891962. Fax: (01392) 438714.
Email: *richard@historicalnovelsociety.org*
Website: *www.historicalnovelsociety.org*

Irish Writers' Union, Irish Writers' Centre, 19 Parnell Square, Dublin 1, Republic of Ireland. Tel: (00 353) 1872 1302. Fax: (00 353) 1872 6282. Email: *info@writerscentre.ie*

New Science Fiction Alliance, Chris Reed, c/o BBR, PO Box 625, Sheffield S1 3GY.
Website: *www.bbr-online.com/catalogue/* support for work of new writers and small presses.

P.E.N. International, for developing friendship and protecting freedom of speech.

English PEN Centre, 6–8 Amwell Street, London EC1R 1UQ. Tel: (020) 7713 0025. Fax: (020) 7837 7838. Email: *enquiries@englishpen.org* Website: *www.englishpen.org*

*The Romantic Novelists' Association, Enquiries: RNA, Coseley House, Munslow, Craven Arms, Shropshire SY7 9ET. Email: *marina@marina-oliver.net*
Website: *www.rna-uk.org/* Offers criticism for unpublished scripts, plus meetings. Publishes newsletter.

Society of Authors, 84 Drayton Gardens, London SW10 9SB. Tel: (020) 7373 6642. Fax: (020) 7373 5768. Email:

info@societyofauthors.org
Website: *www.societyofauthors.org* For professional writers.
Publishes quarterly journal *The Author,* plus guides on
subjects like tax. Meetings and social events.

*Society of Women Writers and Journalists, Broadlea House,
Heron Way, Hickling NR12 0YQ. Tel: (01692) 598 287.
Email: *zoe@zoeking.com* Meetings and advice services.
Publishes quarterly newsletter.

*Women Writers' Network, c/o 23 Prospect Road, London
NW2 2JU. Tel: (020) 7794 5861. Monthly London meetings.
Publishes newsletter and directory.

Writers' Guild of Great Britain, 15 Britannia Street, London
WC1X 9JN. Tel: (020) 7833 0777. Fax: (020) 7833 4777.
Trade union for writers. Email: *admin@writersguild.org*
Website: *www.writersguild.org.uk*

OTHER USEFUL ADDRESSES

Arts Council of England, 14 Great Peter Street, London SW1P
3NQ. Tel: (020) 7333 0100. Fax: (020) 7973 6590.
Website: *www.artscouncil.org.uk/*

Welsh Arts Council, 9 Museum Place, Cardiff CF10 3NX. Tel:
(029) 2037 6500. Fax: (029) 2022 1447.
Website: *www.artswales.org.uk*

Scottish Arts Council, 12 Manor Place, Edinburgh EH3 7DD.
Tel: (0131) 226 6051. Fax: (0131) 225 9833.
Email: *help.desk@scottisharts.org*
Website: *www.scottisharts.org.uk*

N. Ireland Arts Council, MacNiece House, 77 Malone Road,
Belfast BT9 6AQ. Tel: (028) 90038 5200. Fax: (028) 9066
1715. Email: *dsmyth@artscouncil-ni.org*

For Regional Offices see lists in handbooks, or telephone
directories.

The Association of Authors' Agents, c/o A. P. Watt Ltd, 20 John Street, London WC1N 2DR. Tel: (020) 7405 6774. Fax: (020) 7831 2154. Email: *aaa@apwatt.co.uk*
Website: *www.agentsassoc.co.uk* The professional body which has code of practice.

The Authors' Club, 40 Dover Street, London W1X 3RB. Tel: (020) 7499 8581. Fax: (020) 7409 0913.
Email: *secretary@authorsclub.co.uk*
Website: *www.authorsclub.co.uk*

Book Trust, Book House, 45 East Hill, London SW18 2QZ. Tel: (020) 8516 2977. Fax: (020) 8516 2978. Email: *info@booktrust.org.uk* Website: *www.booktrust.org.uk* Masses of information.

British Council, 10 Spring Gardens, London SW1A 2BN. Tel: (020) 7389 3166. Fax: (020) 7839 6347.
Website: *www.britishcouncil.org*

British Library Newspaper Library, Colindale Avenue, London NW9 5HE. Tel: (020) 7412 7353. Fax: (020) 7412 7379. Email: *newspaper@bl.uk* Website: *www.bl.uk/collections/newspaper/*

Department for Culture, Media and Sport, 2–4 Cockspur Street, London SW1Y 5DH. Tel: (020) 7211 6000. Fax: (020) 7211 6270. Email: *lauren.mcgovern@culture.gsi.gov.uk*

National Association of Writers' Groups, The Arts Centre, Biddick Lane, Washington, Tyne and Wear NE38 2AB. Tel: (01262) 609 228. Email: *nawg@tesco.net* Website: *www.nawg.co.uk*

Public Lending Right, Richard House, Sorbonne, Stockton-on-Tees, Cleveland TS17 6DA. Tel: (01642) 604 6099. Fax: (01642) 615 641. Email: *authorservices@plr.com* Website: *www.plr.uk.com* All published books, all editions, should be registered and PLR money is distributed on the basis of library borrowings.

Publishers' Association, 29B Montague Street, London WC1B
5BW. Tel: (020) 7691 9191. Fax: (020) 7691 9199. Email:
mail@publishers.org.uk Website: *www.publishers.org.uk*

Shire Publications Ltd, Cromwell House, Church Street,
Princes Risborough, Buckinghamshire HP27 9AA. Tel:
(01844) 344 301. Fax: (01844) 347 080. Email: *shire@shir-
ebooks.co.uk* Website: *www.shirebooks.co.uk*

StorytrackS Appraisal Agency, 16 St Briac Way, Exmouth,
Devon EX8 5RN. Tel: (01395) 279 659.
Email: *margaret@jamesk.freeserve.co.uk* or
marina@marina-oliver.net Website: *www.storytracks.net*

ADDRESSES IN DIRECTORIES

List of Literature Festivals, The British Council, 10 Spring
Gardens, London SW1A 2BN. Tel: (020) 7395 3166. Fax:
(020) 7839 6347. Website: *www.britishcouncil.org*

Directory of Writers' Circles, Jill Dick, Oldacre, Horderns Park
Road, Chapel en le Frith, Derbyshire SK12 6SY.

CONTACTING THE AUTHOR

Marina Oliver can be contacted on 01584 841 066 or
marina@marina-oliver.net

Further Reading

FURTHER READING

Sample copies of magazines can usually be obtained from the publishers if they are not available through newsagents. Often some contents are available on websites too.

The Author, The Society of Authors, 84 Drayton Gardens, London SW10 9SB. Tel: (020) 7373 6642. Fax: (020) 7373 5768. Email: *info@societyof authors.org*
Website: *www.societyofauthor.org*

The Bookseller, Endeavour House, 5th Floor, 189 Shaftsbury Avenue, London WC2H 8TJ. Tel: (020) 7420 6006. Fax: (020) 7420 6103. Website: *www.thebookseller.com*

Computeractive. A fortnightly magazine in plain English for computer and Internet non-experts. Available on news-stands.

Mslexia, PO Box 656, Newcastle-upon-Tyne NE99 2XD. Tel: (0191) 261 6656. Fax: (0191) 266 6636.
Email: *postbag@mslexia.demon.co.uk*
Website: *www.mslexia.co.uk* A quarterly magazine.

The New Writer, PO Box 60, Cranbrook, Kent TN17 2ZR. Tel: (01580) 212626. Fax: (01580) 212041.
Email: *editor@thenewwriter.com*
Website: *www.thenewwriter.com*

Writers' Forum, PO Box 3229, Bournemouth, Dorset BH1 1ZS. Tel: (01202) 589828. Fax: (01202) 587758.
Email: *editorial@writers-forum.com*
Website: *www.worldwidewriters.com*

Writing Magazine, Writers News, First Floor, Victoria House, 143–144 The Headrow, Leeds LS1 5RL. Tel: (0113) 200 2929. Fax: (0113) 200 2928. Website: *www.writersnews.co.uk*

Writers' News is by subscription, *Writing Magazine* is available on newsstands. Monthly with 'How to' articles, competitions, market news, interviews and reviews.

PUBLISHERS OF REFERENCE BOOKS FOR WRITERS

For addresses not here, see Appendix 2.

Allison & Busby BBC Books, Woodlands, 80 Wood Lane, London W12 0TT. Tel: (020) 8433 2000. Fax: (020) 8423 3707.

A. & C. Black (Publishers Ltd), Alderman House, 37 Soho Square, London W1D 3QZ. Tel: (020) 7758 0200. Fax: (020) 7758 0222. Email: *enquiries@acblack.co.uk*
Website: *www.acblack.com*

BBC Books, Room A3100, BBC Worldwide Ltd, 80 Wood Lane, London W12 0TT. Tel: (020) 8433 2000. Fax: (020) 8749 0538. Website: *www.bbcworldwide.com*

Robert Hale Ltd.

Hodder & Stoughton Educational, Hodder Headline.

How To Books Ltd, 3 Newtec Place, Magdelen Road, Oxford OX4 1RE. Tel: (01865) 793806. Fax: (01865) 248780. Email: *info@howtobooks.co.uk* Website: *www.howtobooks.co.uk*

Piatkus Books.

Routledge, 2 Park Square, Milton Park, Abingdon OX14 4RN. Tel (020) 7017 6000. Fax: (020) 7017 6699. Website: *www.routledge.com*

Studymates Ltd. PO Box 225, Abergele, Conwy County LL18 9AY. Email: *info@studymates.co.uk*

REFERENCE BOOKS – GENERAL ON WRITING AND PUBLISHING

Writers' and Artists' Yearbook, A. & C. Black. Lists publishers and magazines, plus gives advice on various aspects of writing and publishing.

The Writer's Handbook, Barry Turner, Macmillan Reference Books, another yearbook with lists and information.

Writer's Market, The USA Yearbook. Also *Novel and Short Story Writer's Market,* specific to USA fiction markets.

The Author's Handbook, David Bolt, Piatkus Books.

Authors by Profession volume 2, Victor Bonham-Carter, Bodley Head. Volume 1 from the Society of Authors.

Copyright and Law for Writers, Helen Shay, How To Books.

Inside Book Publishing: a career builder's guide, Giles N Clark, Blueprint.

An Author's Guide to Publishing, Michael Legat, Robert Hale.

The Internet: A Writer's Guide, Jane Dormer, A&C Black, 2000.

The Internet Guide for Writers, Malcolm Chisholm, How To Books, 2001.

The Internet for Writers, Nick Daws, Internet Handbooks, 1999.

Publishing and Bookselling in the Twentieth Century, F A Mumby, Unwin Hayman.

The Reading Groups Book, Jenny Hartley, Oxford University Press.

The Ultimate Simple Writer's Guide, Michael Legat, Rosmic Books.

Writer's Guide to Internet Resources, Vicky Phillips and Cindy Yager, Macmillan-USA, 1998.

Using the Internet, Graham Jones, How To Books.

Willings Press Guide, Reed Information Services, Windsor Court, East Grinstead House, East Grinstead, West Sussex RH19 1XA. Information about publishers/magazines/books etc.

DICTIONARY AND THESAURUS PUBLISHERS

There are hundreds to choose from, you can select one to suit your pocket and need. Most publishers produce large, concise, compact, and pocket versions, hard and paperback. The major publishers are:

Cambridge University Press, The Edinburgh Building, Shaftsbury Road, Cambridge CB2 2RU. Tel: (01223) 312 393. Fax: (01223) 315 052.

Cassell Reference, Orion Publishing Group.

HarperCollins Publishers.

Helicon Publishing Ltd, RM plc New Mill House, Milton Park, Abingdon OX14 4SE. Tel: (01235) 826000. Fax: (01235) 823222. Email: *helicon@rm.com*
Website: www.helicon.co.uk

Kingfisher Publications plc, New Penderel House, 283–288 High Holborn, London WC1V 7HZ. Tel: (020) 7903 9999. Fax: (020) 7242 4979. Email: *sales@kingfisherpub.com*

Oxford University Press, Great Clarendon Street, Oxford OX2 6DP. Tel: (01865) 556767. Fax: (01865) 556646. Email: *enquiry@oup.com* Website: *www.oup.com*

Pearson Education, Edinburgh Gate, Harlow, Essex CM20 2JE. Tel: (01279) 623623. Fax: (01279) 431059. Website: *www.pearson.com*

ENCYCLOPEADIAS

The publishers of encyclopeadias often publish concise or pocket editions as well as the larger versions.

The Cambridge Concise encyclopaedias, from Cambridge University Press.

The Guinness encyclopaedias, from Guinness World Records Ltd, 338 Euston Road, London NW1 3BD. Tel: (020) 7891 4567. Fax: (020) 7891 4501.
Email: *info@guinnessrecords.com*
Website: *www.guinnessworldrecords.com*

The Hutchinson encyclopaedias, published by Helicon Publishing.

The Macmillan encyclopaedias.

Pears Cyclopaedia, from Pelham Books, Penguin.

Wordsworth Encyclopaedia, Wordsworth Editions Ltd, 86 East Street, Ware SG12 9HG. Tel: (01920) 465167. Fax: (01920) 462267. Email: *enquiries@wordsworth-editions.com* Website: *www.wordsworth-editions.com*

OTHER REFERENCE BOOKS

This is just a selection, there are many more. Second-hand copies of the annual publications can often be obtained at a fraction of the cost of new editions, and may serve your purposes quite adequately.

Brewer's Concise Dictionary of Phrase and Fable, Helicon.

Brewer's Dictionary of Names, People, Places and Things, Helicon.

Cambridge Biographical Encyclopaedia, Cambridge University Press.

Chambers Biographical Dictionary, Kingfisher.

Chambers Dictionary of Spelling, Kingfisher.

Chambers Dictionary of Synonyms and Antonyms, Kingfisher.

Collins What Happened When, Helicon.

Collins English Spelling Dictionary, Helicon.

Concise Dictionary of English Idioms, B. A. Pythian, Hodder & Stoughton.

Concise Dictionary of English Slang, B. A. Pythian, Hodder & Stoughton.

Concise Dictionary of New Words, B. A. Pythian, Hodder & Stoughton.

Concise Dictionary of Phrase and Fable, B. A. Pythian, Hodder & Stoughton.

Concise Oxford Dictionary of Proverbs, Oxford University Press.

Egon Ronay's Cellnet Guide, Macmillan.

Encyclopaedia of Dates and Events, Teach Yourself Books, Hodder & Stoughton.

Gascoigne Encyclopaedia of Britain, Macmillan.

Good Hotel Guide Britain and Europe, Vermillion.

Hutchinson Dictionary of Biography, Helicon.

Hutchinson Pocket Fact Finder, Helicon.

McNae's Essential Law for Journalists, Walter Greenwood, Butterworth & Co Publishers Ltd.

Oxford Dictionary of Modern Slang, Oxford University Press.

Oxford Dictionary of Quotations, Oxford University Press.

Oxford Dictionary of Slang, Oxford University Press.

Penguin Dictionary of Historical Slang, Eric Partridge, Penguin.

Penguin Dictionary for Writers and Editors, Penguin.

Slang Down the Ages, Jonathon Green, Kyle Cathie.

Whitacker's Almanack, J. Whitaker & Sons Ltd.

Who Was Who, in 9 volumes plus index. A. & C. Black.

Who's Who, A. & C. Black.

Wordsworth Dictionary of Foreign Words in English, John Ayto, Wordsworth Editions Ltd.

ATLASES

Major publishers of atlases, often in conjunction with other publishing houses, are:

AA Publishing
RAC
Philips
Ordnance Survey
A to Z

REFERENCE BOOKS ON PARTICULAR FORMS OF WRITING

Creative Writing and General Books

Awakening the Writer Within, Cathy Birch, How To Books.

Becoming a Writer, Dorothea Brand, Papermac.

The Book Writer's Handbook, Gordon Wells, Allison & Busby, 1991.

The Complete Guide to Writing Fiction, Barnaby Conrad et al, Writer's Digest Books USA, 1990.

Creative Writing, Adèle Ramet, How To Books.

Conflict, Action and Suspense, William Noble.

From Pitch to Publication, Carole Blake, Macmillan, 1999.

Getting into Print, Jenny Vaughan, Bedford Square Press, 1988.

Get Writing, George Evans & Vince Powell, BBC Books, 1990.

How to Get Published, Neil Wenborn, Hamlyn, 1990.

How to Get Published and Make a Lot of Money, Susan Page, Piatkus, 1999.

How to Write Damn Good Fiction, James Frey, Macmillan, 2002.

Is There a Book Inside You? Dan Poynter & Mandy Bingham, Exley, 1988.

On Writing, Stephen King, New English Library, 2000.

Performing Flea, P. G. Wodehouse, Hutchinson, 1953.

Plotting the Novel, Michael Legat, Robert Hale, 1992.

Publishing a Book, Robert Spicer, How To Books.

Research for Writers, Ann Hoffman, A. & C. Black.

Researching for Writers, Marion Field, How To Books.

Revision, Kit Read, Robinson Writer's Workshop, 1991.

Starting to Write, Marina Oliver and Deborah Oliver, Tudor House, 2003.

The Successful Author's Handbook, Gordon Wells, Papermac.

Successful Writing, George Ryley Scott, Lloyd Cole, 1993.

Teach Yourself Creative Writing, Diane Doubtfire, Hodder & Stoughton, 1993.

Twenty Master Plots, Ronald B. Tobias, Piatkus, 1999.

The Way to Write, John Fairfax, Elm Tree.

Ways with Words: BBC Guide to Creative Writing, BBC Books.

Word Power – A Guide to Creative Writing, Julian Birkett, A. &

C. Black.

Writer's Guide to Getting Published, Chriss McCallum, How To Books, 2003.

Writers' Questions Answered, Gordon Wells, Allison & Busby.

The Writer's Rights, Michael Legat, A. & C. Black.

The Writing Business, Liz Taylor, Severn House, 1985.

Writing for a Living, Ian Linton, Kogan Page, 1988.

Writing for Pleasure and Profit, Michael Legat, Robert Hale.

Writing Popular Fiction, Rona Randall, A. & C. Black.

Writing Proposals and Synopses that Sell, André Jute, Writers News.

Writing Step by Step, Jean Saunders, Allison & Busby.

Novels

The Art and Craft of Novel Writing, Oakley Hall, Story Press, USA, 1994.

The Art of Romance Writing, Valerie Parv, Allen & Unwin, 1993.

Bloody Murder, Julian Symons, Penguin, 1985.

The Craft of Novel-Writing, Diane Doubtfire, Allison & Busby.

Crime Writer's Handbook, Douglas Wynn, Allison & Busby.

The Crime Writer's Practical Handbook, John Kennedy (ed.) Melling, Chivers Press.

The Craft of Writing Romance, Jean Saunders, Allison & Busby.

Guide to Fiction Writing, Phyllis Whitney, Poplar Press, 1984.

How to Create Fictional Characters, Jean Saunders, Allison & Busby.

How to Research Your Novel, Jean Saunders, Allison & Busby.

How to Turn Your Holidays into Popular Fiction, Kate Nivison, Allison & Busby.

How to Write a Blockbuster, Sarah Harrison, Allison & Busby, 1995.

How to Write Crime Novels, Isobel Lambot, Allison & Busby.

How to Write a Damn Good Novel, James N. Frey. Papermac.

How to Write Historical Novels, Michael Legat, Allison & Busby.

How to Write a Mi££ion, Dibell, Scott Card & Turco, Robinson Publishing Ltd, 1995.

How to Write Novels, Paddy Kitchen, Elm Tree Books, 1981.

How to Write Realistic Dialogue, Jean Saunders, Allison & Busby.

How to Write Science Fiction, Bob Shaw, Allison & Busby.

How to Write and Sell a Synopsis, Stella Whitelaw, Allison & Busby.

How to Write and Sell Your First Novel, Oscar Collier with Frances Spatz Leighton, Writers' Digest Books, 1995.

Kate Walker's Guide to Writing Romance, Studymates, 2004.

More about How to Write a Mi££ion, Dibell, Scott Card & Turco, Robinson Publishing Ltd, 1996.

Plotting and Writing Suspense Fiction, Patricia Highsmith, Poplar Press, 1983.

Writer's Handbook Guide to Crime Writing, Barry Turner (ed.), Macmillan.

Writer's Handbook Guide to Writing for Children, Barry Turner (ed.), Macmillan.

Writing a Children's Book, Pamela Cleaver, How To Books, 2005.

Writing Comedy, John Byrne, Macmillan.

Writing Crime Fiction, H. R. F. Keating, A. & C. Black, 1987.

Writing Erotic Fiction, Derek Parker, A. & C. Black.

Writing Fantasy and Science Fiction, Lisa Tuttle, Macmillan.

Writing Historical Fiction, Marina Oliver, Studymates, 2005.

Writing Historical Fiction, Rhona Martin, A. & C. Black, 1995.

Writing the Novel from Plot to Print, Lionel Block, Writer's Digest Books, 1979.

Writing Science Fiction, Christopher Evans, A. & C. Black, 1988.

Writing a Thriller, André Jute, A. & C. Black.

Write a Successful Novel, Frederick F. and Moe Sherrard Smith, Escreet Publications, 1991.

To Writers with Love, Mary Wibberley, Buchan & Enright, 1987.

Use of English

Creative Editing, Mary Mackie, Gollancz, 1995.

Effective Grammar, Chambers Paperback.

The Elements of Style, William Strunk Jr. and E. B. White, Macmillan Publishing Co, New York.

Handbook for Written Language, Patricia Gordon, Hodder & Stoughton, 1995.

The Nuts and Bolts of Writing, Michael Legat, Robert Hale.

Oxford Dictionary of English Grammar, Oxford University Press.

Oxford Everyday Grammar, Oxford University Press.

Oxford Guide to Plain English, Martin Cutts, Oxford University Press.

Perfect Punctuation, Chambers Paperback.

Punctuation Made Easy in One Hour, Graham King, Mandarin.

Teach Yourself Correct English, B. A. Phythian, Hodder & Stoughton.

Teach Yourself English Grammar, B. A. Phythian, Hodder & Stoughton.

Write Tight, William Brohaugh, Writer's Digest.

Writer's Descriptive Wordfinder, Barbara Ann Kipfer, Writer's Digest Books.

Index

L

large print, 127, 136

layout, 59, 66, 106

libel, 127

libraries, 4, 13, 27, 28, 45, 50, 75, 85, 119, 120, 123, 124, 130, 132, 134, 136, 137

link, 2, 27

M

magazines, 8, 9, 37, 109, 117, 118, 119, 120, 121, 125, 131, 132, 137

manuscript/script, 8, 44, 55, 58, 59, 60, 62, 65, 102, 106, 107, 108, 110, 112, 113, 115, 118, 119, 122, 123, 128

maps, 27, 75, 86, 137

margins, 60

market, 2, 4, 9, 10, 11, 108, 111, 118, 119, 141

middles, 83, 87, 92, 100

modifiers, 70

multiple submissions, 113

N

names, 28, 35, 36, 37, 56, 68, 86

narrative, 22, 44, 50, 69, 78, 94, 99, 101, 112

networking, 109, 121, 122

newsgroups, 69

notes, 8, 11, 12, 20, 21, 29, 33, 44, 75, 90, 104

O

online, 1, 69, 109, 117, 120, 121, 123, 149

opening, 51, 52, 55, 56

originality, 45, 135

outline, 24, 35, 44, 109, 111

P

pace, 14, 79, 84, 85, 91, 92, 104

padding, 82

paperback, 12, 115, 127, 130, 136

partials, 112

phonetics, 71

plagiarism, 128

planning, 7, 19, 24, 44, 111

plot, 7, 9, 15, 16, 18, 21, 22, 23, 24, 25, 26, 27, 28, 29, 30, 31, 32, 33, 35, 36, 41, 44, 72, 83, 84, 85, 89, 91, 92, 94, 97, 98, 99, 101, 102, 112, 113, 128, 135

polishing, 102

presentation, 58, 59, 110

printer, 8, 60

proofreading, 128, 129

proofs, 129

proposal, 19, 109, 110, 111

protagonist, 31, 32, 33, 38, 39, 41, 42, 47, 48, 90, 100, 101